Grammatical Rules of English

Grammatical Rules of English

In-Seok Yang

Hankook Publishing Co.
Seoul, Korea

First published 2000
Second published 2001
third published 2006
fourth published 2011
fifth published 2014
sixth published 2017

Hankook Publishing Co.
130, Gwangnaru-ro, Seongdong-gu, Seoul, Korea 04788

Phone: (02) 464-7708
Fax: (02) 499-0846
E-mail: hkm77@korea.com
Home-page: www.hankookmunhwasa.co.kr
ISBN: 89-7735-814-0

Contents

Preface

Research is indispensible in any discipline in order to satisfy human desires. Linguistic research satisfies human beings' intellectual desires. However, research without development cannot satisfy human beings' practical desires. That is the reason why research must be followed up by development. Put differently, linguistics has "value" but no "prices". In order to make priceless linguistics a price-bearing discipline, we need development as well. This book is designed to satisfy English learners' practical desires. Naturally, this book is a result of things I've developed for ESL/EFL programs based on linguistic research done mainly by native linguists of English.

Language learning has two routes: inductive and deductive. In the case of native speakers' learning their mother tongue, they implicitly employ an inductive method. They are exposed to item-by-item expressions so that they internalize grammatical rules eventually. On the other hand, in the case of a foreign/second language, adult learners must employ a deductive method. They are supposed to learn rules first and then deductively use the rules in real situations. If foreign/second-language learners could use an inductive method, this book would be out of place. Since they cannot use an inductive method, this book has its price as well as its value.

This book can be used as a textbook for an English grammar or English syntax course at the undergraduate level, as well as at the graduate level. This book is also for English teachers of all levels. Some practical English grammar or usage books are available. They are very useful for foreign/second-language learners of English. However, I feel that many of them have a partial lack of generalizations. With no generalizations can adult non-native speakers internalize the rules. This book has attempted to provide generalizations. One caution must be mentioned. The types of generalizations are over-generalizations, under-generalizations, and optimal generalizations. Since it is difficult to apply over-generalizations in real situations, linguistics books, as they are, cannot be used as textbooks for ESL/EFL programs. On the other hand, learners find it difficult to internalize rules from under-generalizations. Thus, what is required is optimal generalizations, which are the target of this book.

* * *

I appreciate Jeong-Woon Park commenting on the first draft. My graduate students were very cooperative in finding out typos which the context-blind computer cannot check. Wu-Yeal Yoo lent a hand in editing. With my wife's help and encouragement, I could finish this book without hurting my health.

Unit 1

Introduction

This book mainly deals with transformational rules, which were explored and discussed mainly in the 1970s. Since the 1980s, transformational rules have rarely been discussed at linguistic forums. Instead, a variety of theories have attempted to analyze the same phenomena/facts from different perspectives. This change was motivated by linguistic theoretical purposes, but not by pedagogical purposes. In terms of teaching/learning of languages, many of current linguistic theories have little use. Among linguistic theories in terms of rules, the traditional transformation grammar is the best for pedagogical purposes.

In dealing with grammatical rules in this book, formal technicalities are avoided because such technicalities are useless for pedagogical purposes. We can make generalizations without such formal technicalities. The essential necessity of grammatical rules is what I call "alternative expressibility", by which I mean that foreign/second-language learners must have the capability to express one thing in various ways. For instance, they are required to express the same thing in the passive form, as well as in the active form. One might regard the alternative expressibility as going against Bolinger's position: "to reaffirm the old principle that the natural condition of a language is to preserve one form for one meaning and one meaning for one form" (Bolinger 1977:x).

Bolinger's position has been very much respected by many linguists, including me. However, what is not fully agreed upon is the fact that ordinary speakers are not so sensitive to subtle differences in meanings/uses. In this regard, synonymy is divided into full synonymy, cognitive synonymy, and partial synonymy. It is almost impossible for related sentences to have full synonymy. Foreign/second-language learners have to be satisfied mainly with cognitive synonymy, which goes well with alternative expressibility. Related sentences are cognitively synonymous under the condition that if one sentence is true, the other sentence is also true, and vice versa. Related sentences are linked by transformational rules. That is the reason for this book dealing with grammatical rules.

The above paragraph, however, does not mean that partial synonymy is not relevant. Partial synonymy means that two formally related or unrelated sentences/forms have a subtle difference in meaning/use. In linguistic analyses, partial synonymy is most interesting. Subtle differences of meaning/use are also very important to foreign/second-language learners since such differences are required in real situations. For this reason, I sometimes deal with partial synonymy at the relevant places.

Concerning explanations of rules and their constraints, I have attempted to provide "intuitively appealing" ones. That is very important for language learners to internalize rules and their constraints. If the description/explanation is not intuitively appealing, the readers will feel dry, which will not help them to internalize the rules.

Most units deal with grammatical rules, and a few units deal with special constructions. Each rule is followed by relevant constraint(s). The statement "no constraint, no rule" is true. Without constraints, rules are too powerful, which produce even ungrammatical or unacceptable expressions. The literature which deals with rules just mentions their constraints. In contrast, I have attempted to provide "intuitively appealing" reasons concerning constraints.

Each unit ends with "Exercises and problems" of which some problems are not directly mentioned in the body. Such problems are intended for the readers themselves to think about. Some difficult problems can be solved by the assistance of the instructor. This book does not include notes. Whatever deserves to be noted is somehow incorporated in the body.

Unit 2

Adverb-Adjective Attraction

Certain adverbs attract adjectives which are modified by them. That is, closely related adverbs and adjectives are placed side by side. In this sense, the phenomena are reciprocal attractions of adverbs and adjectives. The following illustrate the rule:

(1) a. *John is so a diligent student that everybody likes him.
    b. John is so diligent a student that everybody likes him.

(2) a. *Lincoln was not as a great orator as Douglas.
    b. Lincoln was not as great an orator as Douglas.

(3) a. *This is too a depressing movie to see a second time.
    b. This is too depressing a movie to see a second time.

(4) a. *That is much less a radical claim.
    b. That is much less radical a claim.

In these sentences, if an adverb and an adjective are intervened by an article, they are ungrammatical. In contrast, if they are not intervened, they are grammatical. The rule which derives (b) from (a) is called "Adverb-Adjective Attraction", which means that an adverb attracts an adjective. In this process, the adjective moves over an indefinite article toward the adverb.

It is not the case that any adverb can attract an adjective. To see this restriction, consider the following examples:

(5) a. John is a very good student.
b. *John is very good a student.

(6) a. Smith is an extremely funny man.
b. *Smith is extremely funny a man.

Sentences (5) and (6) are just opposite to sentences (1–4). This contrast suggests that the rule under consideration has a constraint to the effect that adverbs which are relevant are restricted. Emonds (1976:239) indicates that the adverbs are restricted to *as*, *how*, and *too*. However, examples (1) and (4) show that Emonds' restriction is under-generalized. For this reason, I specify the restriction by the following constraint:

(7) Adverb-Adjective Attraction does not apply if the "Art - Adv - Adj - Noun" sequence is well-formed.

This constraint accounts for the ungrammaticalty of the (b) versions of (5) and (6). The reason is very simple. Since the adverb and the adjective are placed side by side, there is no reason for the adverb to attract the adjective. The constraint does not apply to the examples in (1–4):

(8) a. *John is a so diligent student · · ·. (cf. 1)
b. *Lincoln was an as great orator · · ·. (cf. 2)
c. *This is a too depressing movie · · ·. (cf. 3)
d. *That is a much less radical claim · · ·. (cf. 4)

Since these are ungrammatical, Adverb-Adjective Attraction must apply. However, the rule cannot apply to the sentences in (8), because adverbs and adjectives are placed side by side. For the ungrammatical sentences in (8) to be converted to the grammatical (b) sentences in (1–4), the indefinite article must move to the front of the noun. For this reason,

Emonds (1976:238) calls the rule "Article Movement".

Thus, the rule under consideration is called "Adverb-Adjective Attraction" or "Article Movement". This difference, however, is not accidental. If we regard the (a) structures of (1–4) as the sources for the rule, "Adverb-Adjective Attraction" is appropriate. In contrast, if we regard the structures in (8) as the sources for the rule, "Article Movement" is appropriate. Furthermore, their perspectives are different. The former is the functionally motivated name, while the latter is the structurally motivated name.

Consider the following examples from Emonds (1976:239):

(9) a. *A how young kitten is able to go outside?
    b. How young a kitten is able to go outside?

(10) a. *John is an as nice boy as you will find.
    b. John is as nice a boy as you will find.

(11) a. *This is a too depressing movie to see a second time.
    b. This is too depressing a movie to see a second time.

These data are also accounted for by the constraint in (7). Since the adverbs cannot occur in their present positions, the rule must apply to the (a) versions in order to derive the grammatical (b) versions.

Next consider the following:

(12) a. *They are <u>so diligent students</u> that everybody likes them.
    b. They are <u>such diligent students</u> that everybody likes them.

Sentence (12a) is ungrammatical, while sentence (12b) is grammatical. This shows that there is a serious difference between *so* and *such*. The contrast of them is this: *so* is not compatible with nouns, whereas *such* is compatible only with nouns. This difference is also confirmed by the following examples:

(13) a. *They were not prepared for so cold weather.
b. They were not prepared for such cold weather.

The ungrammaticality of (13a) is due to the fact that the adverb *so* is used with a noun, "*(cold) weathe*r". In contrast, the grammaticality of (13b) is due to the fact that *such* occurs with a noun. The contrast of *so* and *such* is as follows:

(14) Contrast of *so* and *such*
a. *So* is not compatible with NPs, but with APs.
b. *Such* is compatible only with NPs.

This means that *so* is an adverb, whereas *such* is not an adverb.

The following illustrate possible combinations in the case of more than one adjective:

(15) a. He is a tall honest student.
b. He is so tall honest a student.
c. He is so tall an honest student.
d. He is so honest a tall student.
e. He is so tall and honest a student.
f. He is such a tall honest student.

(16) a. They are tall honest students.
b. *They are so tall honest students.
c. *They are so tall and honest students.
d. They are such tall honest students.
e. They are such tall and honest students.

I do not explain each case of the above examples, simply because the generalized contrast of *so* and *such* in (14) can account for them.

The following examples are interesting:

(17) a. This/That tall boy is good for basketball.
b. This/That tall a boy is good for basketball.

Interestingly enough, *this/that tall boy* means *this/that boy*, but *this/that tall a boy* does not mean *this/that boy*. Why is it? The answer requires the notion of "deixis". In (17a), *this/that* functions like a definite article, in addition to the deictic function. In (17b), in contrast, *this/that* functions like an adverb, in addition to the deictic function. In other words, the deictic elements, *this* and *that*, function as determiners in (17a), and as adverbs in (17b).

Compare the following sentences:

(18) a. This/That tall a student is not good for basketball.
b. This/That rude a student does not irritate teachers.

In (18a), *this/that tall a student* can imply *a short student*; in (18b), in contrast, *this/that rude a student* cannot imply *a polite student*. This difference hinges on the contrast of the neutralizable antonym pair *tall and short* and the non-neutralizable antonym pair *polite and rude*. For details, see Yang (1993f).

The adverbial question word *how* naturally attracts adjectives and adverbs:

(19) a. *How is Bill sane?
b. How sane is Bill?

(20) a. *How have you picked up TNT carelessly?
b. How carelessly have you picked up TNT?

(21) a. *How a strong worker are you looking for?
b. How strong a worker are you looking for?

(22) a. *How a bright assistant are you looking for?
b. How bright an assistant are you looking for?

While reading a book, I noticed (23a), but the (23b, c) versions are not grammatical:

(23) a. The preparation of the final manuscript from all these efforts was <u>no less onerous a task</u> than the organization of the conference itself, partly because . . . (source: Ortony (ed.), *Metaphor and Thought*, viii)
b. *. . . no less an onerous task . . .
c. *. . . a no less onerous task . . .

The contrast between (22a) and (22b, c) is clear, and they can be accounted for by the reasons thus far indicated.

Exercises and problems

1. What is the difference of *it*, *so* and *such* with respect to Adverb Adjective Attraction?
2. What is the perspective difference between "Adverb-Adjective Attraction" and "Article Movement"?
3. Provide evidence that *such* and *it* are not adverbs.
4. What is the syntactic category of *such*?
5. Why is it that *this/that tall a boy* does not mean *this/that boy*?

6. Describe the deixis system of your mother tongue, and compare it with that of English.
7. Specify the situations where the following sentences are distinctively used:
    a. I am John Smith.
    b. This is John Smith. (this = I)
8. Draw some generalization from the following data:

    *a so good boy, so good a boy, *a such good boy, such a good boy, *so good boys, such good boys

Unit 3

Though Attraction

This rule is also known as *Though* Inversion or *Though* Preposing. The following illustrate the rule (cf. Culicover 1982):

(1) a. Though the house is expensive, we have decided to buy it.
  b. Expensive though the house is, we have decided to buy it.

(2) a. Though John is a genius, he can't tie his shoe laces.
  b. *A genius though John is, he can't tie his shoe laces.
  c. Genius though John is, he can't tie his shoe laces.

In (1b), what is attracted/preposed is an adjective. (2b) and (2c) show that a noun can be attracted/preposed only without a determiner; it is known that a determiner or a quantifier cannot accompany a noun in the process of *Though* Attraction. While reading an article, I noticed the following example, which supports the claim that a noun can be attracted/preposed only without a determiner:

(3) a. Supporter though I be of radically pragmatic analyses in logical and linguistic semantics, I have always been unhappy with Geach's logical analysis of the truth-conditions of *only* sentences.
  (source: *Journal of Semantics* 10.4:303)

It seems that if the rule attracts a noun, the noun must become a bare noun. Then, a natural question is: what is the difference between "a determinered noun" and "a bare noun"? Suppose that only adjectivals can be freely attractable/preposable by *Though* Attraction. On this assumption, we can say that the best way for nouns to become adjectives is to become bare nouns. The source of (3a) is (3b) below:

(3) b. Though I am a supporter of radically pragmatic analyses in logical and linguistic semantics, . . .

The following examples show whether preposition phrases (PPs) can be attracted:

(4) a. Though the book was on the table, I couldn't find it.
b. ?On the table though the book was, I couldn't find it.

(5) a. Though the concert is in June, we decided to buy the tickets now.
b. *?In June though the concert is, we decided to buy the tickets now.

(6) a. Though John was running down the stairs, they made no attempt at silence.
b. *Running down the stairs though John was, they made no attempt at silence.
c. *Running though John was down the stairs, they made no attempt at silence.

Examples (4) and (5) show that PP is very marginal at best. In fact, the syntactic category PP has the nature of Janus: in other words, some PPs have the function of adjective phrases (APs). The function of adjectival PPs is equivalent to that of APs. For example, the PP *of interest* is an adjectival PP, which means *interesting*. Adjectival PPs can undergo *Though* Attraction.

(7) a. Though the book is interesting, it doesn't sell well.
b. Interesting though the book is, it doesn't sell well.

(8) a. Though the book is of interest, it doesn't sell well.
b. %Of interest though the book is, it doesn't sell well.

Concerning (8b) where an adjectival PP is involved, some speakers do not accept it. This suggests that whether adjectival PPs behave like APs in *Though* Attraction seems to be subject to idiolectal variation.

The underlined PPs in (4) and (5) are not adjectival PPs. Hence, (4b) and (5b) are not fully grammatical. Examples in (6) show that the present participle cannot be attracted. Thus far, we can see that only adjectivals are freely attracted. The following examples support this tentative generalization:

(9) a. Though Fred was intimidated by Mary, he stood his ground.
b. <u>Intimidated</u> by Mary though Fred was, he stood his ground.
c. <u>Intimidated</u> though Fred was by Mary, he stood his ground.

(10) a. Though the soldiers were tired, they were forced to march to the end of the land.
b. <u>Tired</u> though the soldiers were, they were forced to march to the end of the land.

(11) a. Though John is gone, his charisma is still influential among the followers.
b. <u>Gone</u> though John is, his charisma is still influential among the followers.

The (b) versions are grammatical only in the stative sense of the underlined past participles. This means that the past participles are similar to adjectives. Thus, a tentative generalization is:

(12) <u>Tentative generalization</u>
The attractable elements by *Though* Attraction are adjectivals.

Here, adjectivals refer to adjectives and their equivalents.

A relevant question is: why it is that present participles (cf. 6) are not attractable, while past participles (cf. 9-11) are attractable. One possible explanation is this. Past participles are closer to adjectives, whereas present participles are closer to verbs. This explanation, however, has a weakness, because VPs are attractable, as shown below. Hence, the adequate explanation is not available.

VPs can also be attracted by *Though* Attraction. (This is not VP Preposing which will be discussed in unit 10.)

(13) a. Though John ate the meat singing/shouting, nobody thought he was crazy.
b. Eat the meat singing/shouting though John did, nobody thought he was crazy.

(14) a. Though Andy will attack Clinton, he won't vote against the government.
b. Attack Clinton though Andy will, he won't vote against the government.

Thus, the tentative generalization must be revised as follows:

(15) Generalization

The attractable elements by *Though* Attraction are:

(i) Adjectival and (ii) VP

A serious question here is: what makes adjectivals and VPs a natural class with respect to *Though* Attraction? The answer calls for research.

Exercises and problems

1. Can a noun be attracted/preposed by *Though* Attraction? If yes, on what condition?
2. Do VPs behave like adjectivals in *Though* Attraction?
3. Justify the claim that past participles behave like adjectives.
4. What is the function of *Though* Attraction?
5. Which is the correct *though*-attracted one (i.e. which is the ungrammatical one)?
    a. Although Dick is handsome, I'm still going to marry John.
    b. Handsome though Dick is, I'm still going to marry John.
    c. Handsome although Dick is, I'm still going to marry John.
6. What is the difference of *although* and *though*?
7. Discuss whether *gone* is a past participle or an adjective in the following sentences.
    a. He is gone.
    b. Gone are the days when I was young and gay.
8. Suppose that (8b) is not grammatical. Then, how must the generalization in (15) be adjusted?
9. Which is/are acceptable?
    a. Although, I like the proposal that "English" must be replaced by "Worldish".
    b. Though, I like the proposal that ⋯.
    c. I like the proposal that ⋯, although.
    d. I like the proposal that ⋯, though.

Unit 4

Placement of Adverbials

One of the difficult problems is where an adverbial must be placed in a sentence. One distributional restriction is this: no adverbial element (sentential adv. and VP adv.) can occur between a predicate and an NP object, although it often can occur between a predicate and a complement clause object (cf. Dixon 1991:25-26):

(1) VP adverbials
  a. John carefully examined the problem.
  b. John examined the problem carefully.
  c. *John examined carefully the problem.

(2) Sentential adverbials
  a. Yesterday I remembered the applicant.
  b. I remembered the applicant yesterday.
  c. *I remembered yesterday the applicant.

One interesting question is why adverbials are not allowed especially between a predicate and an NP object. I think there must be some reason: a predicate and its object make a coherent constituent, VP. Figuratively speaking, nothing can easily break into a nutshell, a snailshell, or a turtleback.

Consider the following examples, keeping the nutshell hypothesis in mind:

(3) a. Yesterday I remembered that I saw Mary the day before yesterday.

b. ?I remembered that I saw Mary the day before yesterday, yesterday.
c. I remembered yesterday that I saw Mary the day before yesterday.

In (3), the VP constituent is made of a predicate and a sentential complement object. (2c) and (3c) have similar structures. However, (2c) is ungrammatical, while (3c) is grammatical. This fact rejects the nutshell hypothesis. The only difference between (2c) and (3c) is that the NP object of (2c) is non-heavy (= light), while the sentential complement object of (3c) is heavy. In (3), the adverb, *yesterday*, modifies the main clause; in (3a) the distance between the modifier and the modified is close, while the distance in (3b) is not close enough. In this sense, (3b) is less acceptable, although grammatical. In this situation, (3c) is the dark horse. This dark horse is the product of the saying that necessity is the mother of invention. Thus, the nutshell hypothesis must give priority to the necessity hypothesis. In short, necessity allows an adverb to break into the VP constituent. In this case, the adverb is usually preceded and followed by a comma. (This is the power of comma, which cannot be ignored in language use as well as in linguistic analyses.)

There are cases in which an adverb "is forced" to be placed between verb and NP object ("forced insertion"):

(4) a. I always hate to visit again cities that I visited before.
b. I always hate to visit cities that I visited again before.

In (4a), an adverb occurs between verb and object; this is a case of the "forced insertion" because if that adverb is placed as in (4b), that adverb modifies the complement clause, but not the main clause. This phenomenon is connected with adverbial modification:

(5) a. John and Mary made $20,000 together.

b. John and Mary together made $20,000.
c. Together, John and Mary made $20,000.

(5a) means that John and Mary participated in some joint enterprise, which earned them $20,000. (5b) and (5c) mean that John and Mary's combined income was $20,000. (Technically, the matter of adverbial modification is treated in terms of scope ambiguity, in semantics.)

Consider the following examples from Rosenbaum (1967:66–67):

(6) a. I want John to go very much.
b. *I want for John to go very much.
c. *I want very much John to go.
d. I want very much for John to go.

We are now to explain the difference of grammaticality of these sentences. First, compare (6a) and (6b). The underlined adverbial modifies *I want*. The structural difference of these sentences is seemingly the presence and the absence of the infinitival complementizer *for*. (6a) has a single clause, which contains subject, verb, object, object complement, and adverb. Since these elements in (6a) are clause mates (i.e. elements within a clause boundary), the adverb *very much* can modify the main verb *want*. Hence, sentence (6a) is grammatical. In contrast, (6b) has a complex sentence: the main clause *I want*, and the infinitival complement *for John to go*. Elements in one clause and elements in another clause are not clause mates. Hence, the adverb *very much*, which is in an infinitival complement clause, cannot modify the verb *want*, which is in the main clause. For this reason, the adverb *very much* is forced to modify its clause mate *go*, which becomes *go very much*. This combination is semantically awkward. Hence, sentence (6b) is ungrammatical.

Next, compare (6c) and (6d). In (6c), the adverb modifies its clause-mate verb *want*, but it is placed between the verb *want* and its object *John*; this is not a proper placement of an adverb. Hence, sentence (6c) is not grammatical. Sentence (6d) has a complex sentence, like (6b). The adverb *very much* modifies its clause-mate verb *want*. Here in (6d), the adverb is not placed between verb and its object, because *for John to go* is not the verb's clause-mate object, but its non-clause-mate object. Hence, sentence (6d) is grammatical (cf. Unit 19).

The sentences in (6) look very simple. Our proper understanding of them, however, is not possible without our proper understanding of placement of adverbs. This is the reason that I deal with placement of adverbials in this book.

Sentence adverbs such as *evidently, frankly* and *probably* occur in all possible positions as a daughter of S, namely, initial, final, before Aux and after first Aux, but not after subsequent ones (cf. Jackendoff 1977:48). Especially, it should be emphasized that, in the case of Aux, adverbs occur before or after the first Aux element, when there are more than one Aux element:

(7) a. George <u>frankly</u> will have amused the children by the time we get there.
    b. George will <u>frankly</u> have amused the children by the time we get there.
    c. *George will have *frankly* amused the children by the time we get there.

For the distinction of sentence adverbs and VP adverbs, see McCawley (1988:631-640).

While reading books and articles, I noticed the following examples, in which an adverb is placed between "X and Y". Here, the two elements (X and Y) are very closely related. Readers will see that each placement of the adverb is rather a forced insertion:

(8) a. This meaning must be due largely to the constraint mentioned above.
b. Let us return once again to the rape passage to emphasize . . .
c. I want now to introduce the notion of non-propositional meaning.
d. Our perceptions of significance are subject, in a large degree, to the influence of personalities and the whims of fashion.
e. The difference in form will correspond in some way to the difference in meaning.
f. I have been interested for a long time in words whose grammatical and semantic properties struck me as being completely unique.
g. Our proposals will extend correctly to dative passive constructions.
h. Ability to undergo Dative Shift depends crucially on the directional content of the role assigned to indirect object.
i. Let us look more closely at the body-part possessor ascension alternation.
j. If the syntactic properties of a verb indeed follow in large part from the meaning, . . .
k. Argument structures might in turn be derived to a large extent from the meaning of words.
l. The initial problems for the matter relate, directly or indirectly, to the sentential complement clause.
m. This follows in these authors' terms from the fact that . . .
n. I am unable at this point to propose a satisfactory analysis of un-passives.
o. We search worldwide for the best products of . . .

Through these examples, we see that the underlined parts are inserted between X and Y, which are somehow very closely related.

Inserted adverbials may be "commaed". If the inserted material is rather long, the use of commas is required in order to signal that X and Y are linked although the inserted material belongs to neither X nor Y. As mentioned above, the insertions of adverbs between X and Y are rather forced ones. It should be noted that the forced insertion in general is not restricted to adverbials. A special type of forced insertions is the "split infinitive" (cf. Quirk *et al* 1985:496–498).

Exercises and problems

1. Specify the conditions for placement of adverbials between a predicate and its NP object.
2. How do we distinguish between sentence adverbs and VP adverbs?
3. Figure out some sentences, where an adverb may be placed in different positions and it modifies different elements.
4. Describe scope phenomena, in which adverbs are involved.
5. Find out "forced insertions", with respect to adverbials and other materials.
6. Why is it that adverbials may be rather easily placed between predicates and complement clause objects, while they are not allowed between predicates and NP objects, except for forced insertions?

Unit 5

Topicalization

An element may be picked up from a sentence and be placed to the front of it. This element is called "topic", which is what is talked about the sentence. That is, a sentence may have a topic, which is called "sentence topic". A paragraph may have a sentence which functions as a topic, which is called "paragraph topic". A discourse may also have a sentence which functions as a topic, which is called "discourse topic". The paragraph and discourse topics are not required to be necessarily placed to their fronts, unlike sentence topics. Here we deal with only sentence topics. The rule which links a sentence and its topicalized sentence is called Topicalization, or Y-movement (Y stands for Yiddish).

In each of the following pairs, the rule links (a) and (b):

(1) a. I used to fly this kite with my brother in winter.
    b This kite$_{(,)}$ I used to fly [e] with my brother in winter.

(2) a. John examined each question carefully.
    b. Each question$_{(,)}$ John examined [e] carefully.

(3) a. We are proud of our ancestors with respect to wisdom.
    b. Our ancestors$_{(,)}$ we are proud of [e] with respect to wisdom.

(4) a. Bill tried to memorize the poem before the next class.
    b. The poem$_{(,)}$ Bill tried to memorize [e] before the next class.

(5) a. Cancer has killed the eminent scientist, unfortunately.
    b. The eminent scientist$_{(,)}$ cancer has killed [e], unfortunately.

In the above examples, Topicalization preposes NP, which is optionally followed by a comma. The extracted site is marked by "[e]".

This rule may prepose not only NP but also AP (in Yiddish English), PP, and S (cf. Jackendoff 1977:42):

(6) a. No one ever expected you to be taller than Bill.
   b. Taller than Bill$_{(,)}$ no one ever expected you to be [e].

(7) a. We asked you to put the bananas into the basket.
   b. Into the basket$_{(,)}$ we asked you to put the bananas [e].

(8) a. No one ever expected Bill to find out that you were coming.
   b. That you were coming$_{(,)}$ no one ever expected Bill to find out [e].

Curiously enough, out of the major syntactic categories, only VP cannot be topicalized:

(9) a. No one ever expected Bill to find out that you were coming tomorrow.
   b. *Coming tomorrow$_{(,)}$ no one ever expected Bill to find out that you were [e].

In an appropriate context, however, VP may be preposed. This rule is called VP Preposing, which will be dealt with in a separate unit, Unit 10.

Topicalization, according to Borkin (1984:84–85), can move the subject of a sentential complement in which the complementizer *that* is omitted:

(10) a. I believe that Mary is genuinely ill, but I believe that John is only fooling.
   b. *Mary, I believe that [e] is genuinely ill, but John, I believe that [e] is only fooling.

(11) a. I believe Mary is genuinely ill, but I believe John is only fooling.
b. Mary, I believe [e] is genuinely ill, but John, I believe [e] is only fooling.

She further indicates that the object of a sentential complement can be moved to the front from *that*-less complements more easily than from complements in which *that* is not omitted:

(12) a. I suppose that you'll want to wear this dress.
b. ?This dress, I suppose that you'll want to wear [e].

(13) a. I suppose you'll want to wear this dress.
b. This dress, I suppose you'll want to wear [e].

Through examples (10–13), we can see that the sentential complementizer *that* plays a significant role, in allowing or not allowing an element to be extracted from its complement. In the case in which *that* is not omitted, the main clause (e.g. *I believe/suppose*) cannot be parenthetically understood. In the case in which *that* is omitted, in contrast, the main clause can be parenthetically understood. This difference is reflected in the degree of grammaticality of the topicalized versions above (cf. Complement Preposing in Unit 22). In some other units, we will see that the presence or absence of the complementizer *that* plays an important role.

Consider the following examples from Jacobson (1990):

(14) a. I like my tea to be hot; I like my beer to be cold.
b. *To be hot, I like my tea [e]; to be cold, I like my beer [e].

(15) a. I like my tea hot; I like my beer cold.
b. ?Hot, I like my tea [e]; cold, I like my beer [e].

The slight difference between (14b) and (15b), with respect to the degree of ungrammaticality, is the difference of the presence and the absence of *to be*. For this difference, a functional explanation is called for. In (14b), the initial infinitive clause possibly takes the subject function, and then it cannot be linked to the "[e]". Hence, (14b) is not grammatical. In (15b), the initial adjective cannot take the subject function. Therefore, it must be linked to "[e]". That is, the initial adjective has a function in the sentence, like (15a). Hence, (15b) is better than (14b).

The following is an example of Resumptive (Clause) Topicalization (cf. Haiman 1985:55):

(16) He sat down. Having sat down, he undid his tie.

The second sentence begins by repeating the content of the first sentence. The repeated part, which is underlined, functions as a topic. The repeating of the content of the preceding sentence is called "resumptive". Hence, this topicalization is called Resumptive (Clause) Topicalization.

We must remember the expression: "no constraint, no rule". Any rule has some constraint(s). In the case of Topicalization, in addition to the constraints mentioned above, indefinite NPs cannot be topicalized. This restriction is not accidental, since topics carry known/old information. This rule will be further discussed in conjunction with Left-Dislocation in the next unit.

Exercises and problems

1. Pick up any paragraph, and find out its topic sentence.
2. Can Topicalization apply to the embedded sentence? Justify your answer.
3. Is a comma required after the topic?
4. Gundel (1977:134) mentions two types of topicalization: (i) Focus topicalization, which is derived from the corresponding cleft sentence. The topicalized NP has primary stress. And (ii) topic topicalization, which is derived from the corresponding left-dislocated sentence. The topicalized NP does not have primary stress. Illustrate the two types of topicalization.
5. It is generally claimed that the particles *nɨn/ɨn* in Korean, and the Japanese counterpart *wa* are topic markers. Justify your position on this claim.
6. Why is it that the focused element is fronted in a sentence? How about the paragraph topic sentence? Is it restricted to the paragraph-initial position?

Unit 6

Left-Dislocation and Right-Dislocation

Left-Dislocation

Quite similarly to Topicalization, Left-Dislocation may front an NP from a sentence. In this process, a comma follows the left-dislocated NP, and the dislocated NP leaves its pronominal trace, unlike the case of Topicalization. The following illustrate the rule:

(1) a. This room really depresses the students.
    b. This room, it really depresses the students.

(2) a. John's brother won't do anything radical.
    b. John's brother, he won't do anything radical.

(3) a. I bought these books at the university bookstore.
    b. These books, I bought them at the university bookstore.

(4) a. I told you you wouldn't like this show much.
    b. This show, I told you you wouldn't like it much.

(5) a. I would marry Harry's pretty sister, when she becomes 25.
    b. Harry, I would marry his pretty sister, when she becomes 25.

This rule also has some constraints. Indefinite NPs and WH-words cannot be left-dislocated (Bach 1974:256):

(6) a. I saw a plumber yesterday.
b. *A plumber, I saw him yesterday.

(7) a. I saw whom yesterday?
b. *Who, I saw him yesterday?

The impossibility of fronting indefinite NPs and WH-words is the same both in Topicalization and in Left-Dislocation. This suggests that the two rules share much of their functions. In fact, however, Bach's restriction is too strong (cf. Gundel 1977:51–54). Left-Dislocation can apply to indefinite NPs, in which the pronominal trace is *one/ones:*

(8) a. Sue wants to marry an honest politician.
b. *An honest politician, Sue wants to marry him.
c. An honest politician, Sue wants to marry one.

(8b) is ungrammatical since the left-dislocated indefinite NP does not agree with the definite pronominal trace. In contrast, (8c) is grammatical since the left-dislocated indefinite NP agrees with the indefinite pronominal trace. The pronoun *one* can have a specific or non-specific reading:

(9) a. Sue wants to marry an honest politician.
b. An honest politician, Sue wants to marry one. His name is Goodfellow.
c. An honest politician, Sue wants to marry one; but she hasn't been able to find one.

In (9b), the pronoun *one* is specific since it is specifically indicated by the name. In contrast, in (9c), the pronoun *one* is non-specific since *one* remains *one* in the following sentence.

Left-Dislocation cannot front head nouns of complex NPs (Grosu 1974):

(10) a. I have met the boy who was wearing a hat.
b. *The boy, I have met him who was wearing a hat.

(11) a. I believe the claim that cybernation will replace many a human worker.
b. *The claim, I believe it that cybernation will replace many a human worker.

Head nouns of complex NPs have two sources: one is head nouns of relative clauses, and the other is head nouns of content clauses. (10) is an example of the former, and (11) is an example of the latter. A complex NP refers to an NP followed by a relative clause or a content clause (cf. Yang 1993d:111–162). In contrast, a simplex NP refers to an NP not followed by such a clause. For content clauses and relative clauses, see Unit 11.

One important formal difference between Topicalization and Left-Dislocation is that the former is a chopping rule while the latter is a copying rule. That is, a chopping rule does not leave its pronominal trace, while a copying rule leaves its pronominal trace. This formal difference is also reflected with respect to Island Constraints, which means that a rule cannot extract any element which is in an island (cf. Ross 1986:271–288). Notions of island and island constraints can be easily understood through concrete examples. Island Constraints include Complex NP Constraint (CNPC), Sentential Subject Constraint (SSC), Coordinate Structure Constraint (CSC).

The following illustrate CNPC:

(12) a. The lawyer acknowledged that the technician erased some tapes.
b. What tapes did the lawyer acknowledge that the technician erased [e]?

(13) a. The lawyer acknowledged the fact that the technician erased some tapes.

b. *What tapes did the lawyer acknowledge the fact that the technician erased [e]?

In (12), in the process of changing (a) to (b) by Wh-question, *some tapes* is extracted from a simplex NP (sentential complement = *that*-complement). (12b) is well-formed/grammatical because Wh-question does not violate CNPC. In (13), however, in the same process, *some tapes* is extracted from a complex NP (a head noun and a content clause). (13b) is ill-formed/ungrammatical because Wh-question violates CNPC. Figuratively speaking, the head noun functions as a gate-guard. This special guard never allows anybody to get out of the building. If somebody gets out of it despite the rigorous rule, the guard gives him/her a punch in the face, which causes a flashing star in his/her eyes. This happening results in a starred sentence, which conventionally marks the sentence's ungrammaticality.

Now consider the following examples:

(14) a. Seoul makes the claim that X broke the promise.

b. What does Seoul make the claim that X broke [e]?

(14a) has a complex NP (head noun and content clause), which meets the requirement of CNPC. (14b), however, is grammatical, which calls for explanation. Any structural/formal explanation is not available. There is only one alternative, which is a semantic explanation. The VP *make the claim* semantically means just a verb *claim*. Hence, (14a) is semantically equivalent to (14a') below:

(14) a'. Seoul claims that X broke the promise.

The object NP of this sentence is not a complex NP but a simplex NP. Thus, (14a) and (14a') escape CNPC. This explanation is not a structural/ formal one but a semantic one.

This fact strongly suggests that analyses of syntactic phenomena require semantic factors as well as syntactic factors. Two rival views on this matter are: the autonomy of syntax and the non-autonomy of syntax. The former claims that "semantics begins where syntax ends" whereas the latter claims that "syntax may need semantic factors". The data just discussed above supports the non-autonomy. This position will be further supported with CSC to be discussed later.

Returning to the data in (13), (13b) is blocked from being well-formed/ grammatical. Such a blocking is a structural blocking, which means that the blocking is due to the nature of structure itself. In comparison with structural blocking, there is lexical blocking, which means that the ill- formedness/ungrammaticality of a sentence is not due to the nature of the structure but due to the nature of the word. Lexical blocking will be discussed in some other units.

The following illustrate the Sentential Subject Constraint (SSC), which means that "an NP that is part of a sentential subject NP cannot be extracted". Relativization and Question Formation are relevant rules.

(15) a. The reporters expected that the principal would fire <u>some teacher</u>.
b. The teacher who the reporters expected that the principal would fire [e] is an idle one.

(16) a. That the principal would fire <u>some teacher</u> was expected by the reporters.
b. *The teacher who that the principal would fire [e] was expected by the reporters is an idle one.

(17) a. It was expected by the reporters that the principal would fire some teacher.
b. The teacher who it was expected by the reporters that the principal would fire [e] is an idle one.

In (15), in the process of relativization, the extracted element *some teacher* is from the sentential object (which is a simplex NP), but not from the sentential subject. Hence, (15b) is well-formed. In (16), the extracted element *some teacher* is from a sentential subject (which is a simplex NP). Hence, (16b) is ill-formed because it violates SSC. In (17), the extracted element *some teacher* is not from a sentential subject; the subject of (17a) is *it*. Hence, (17b) is well-formed. Functionally speaking, the ill-formedness of (16b) is due to the fact that the antecedent *the teacher* has two relative pronouns, *who* and *that*, so that the parsing is confusing.

The following illustrate the Coordinate Structure Constraint (CSC), which means that "an NP that is a conjunct of a coordinate structure cannot be extracted":

(18) a. We have to read some books and some papers.
b. *Which books do we have to read [e] and some papers?
c. *Those are the papers that we have to read some books and [e].

In (18a), the sequence of *some books and some papers* is a coordinate structure. In (18b), only the first conjunct is extracted in the process of Question Formation, while in (18c) only the second conjunct is extracted in the process of Relativization. Both (18b) and (18c) are ill-formed because they violate CSC. Functionally speaking, the symmetric structure does not allow asymmetric change.

As mentioned above in the discussion of CNPC, here again the matter of autonomy vs. non-autonomy of syntax becomes an issue. CSC cannot apply across the board; there are coordinate structures which do not obey CSC:

(19) a. Harry went to the store and bought some whiskey.
b. What did Harry go to the store and buy [e]?

(20) a. You can drink some and still stay sober.
b. How much can you drink [e] and still stay sober?

The (a) sentences have coordinate structures. Hence, they are expected to obey CSC. Nonetheless, as the (b) sentences show, they don't obey the constraint. The autonomy theory of syntax cannot explain this phenomenon. The two conjuncts in each of the (a) sentences are pragmatically closely related; the two conjuncts make a coherent series of one event. It is known that CSC may be violated when the two conjuncts are linked by the meaning of *despite* or *in order to*. The proper understanding/analysis of these sentences requires some pragmatic factor, which supports the non-autonomy of syntax (cf. Goldsmith 1985, Ross 1986, Lakoff 1986).

Now that the background is clarified, we are ready to describe the difference between Topicalization and Left-dislocation with respect to Island Constraints. To put the conclusion first, Topicalization is subject to these constraints, whereas Left-dislocation is not (cf. Ross 1986:256). For example, in the case of CNPC:

(21) a. The lawyer acknowledged the fact that the technician erased some tapes. (complex NP involved)
b. Some tapes, the lawyer acknowledged the fact that the technician erased them. (Left-dislocation)
c. *Some tapes the lawyer acknowledged the fact that the technician erased [e]. (Topicalization)

If we apply Left-dislocation to (21a) where a complex NP is involved, the resultant sentence (21b) is grammatical. In contrast, if we apply Topicalization to the same sentence (21a), the resultant sentence (21c) is ungrammatical. What makes this difference? Structurally speaking, Left-dislocation is a copying rule, whereas Topicalization is a chopping rule. This formal explanation is an explanation. But with this formal explanation, the initial question, what makes this difference?, still remains unanswered. Functionally speaking, the left-dislocated sentence keeps the original information, whereas the topicalized sentence doesn't, which causes the parsing to be difficult.

This matter also shows us that linguistic explanations must not be confined only to structural ones; if necessary, functional and/or semantic and/or pragmatic information must be evoked.

Right-Dislocation

This rule is similar to Left-dislocation, except for the moving direction. The following illustrate the rule:

(22) a. John's big cigar really bothers me.
b. It really bothers me, John's big cigar.

(23) a. The old man visits this park every day.
b. The old man visits it every day, this park.

(24) a. I told you you wouldn't like this movie much.
b. I told you you wouldn't like it much, this movie.

Left-dislocation and Right-dislocation have different functions. As already indicated above, the left-dislocated element functions as a topic.

The right-dislocated element, in contrast, does not do such a function; instead, it expresses the speaker's after-thought. That is, the speaker is afraid that the hearer might have missed the pronoun. In cases like this, the speaker adds the original nominal.

Exercises and problems

1. Which do you prefer, autonomy or non-autonomy of syntax? Justify your position.
2. Name chopping rules and copying rules.
3. Are Island Constraints universal, typological, or language specific?
4. What are other leftward movement rules, and what are other rightward movement rules?
5. Is there any functional difference between the topicalized element and the left-dislocated element?
6. Compare the main points of Topicalization and Left-dislocation.
7. Both the topicalized NP and the left-dislocated NP may be preceded by expressions such as *about*, *as for*, or *concerning*. Then what is the functional difference of the two rules?
8. Why is it that Topicalization applies to NP, AP, PP, and S, whereas Left-dislocation applies only to NP?
9. How does Left-dislocation behave when it applies to indefinite NPs?
10. Is one which is left behind by indefinite NP in the process of Left-dislocation specific, non-specific, or either?
11. Out of Island Constraints, which is/are practically useful?
12. Suppose little ants bother the owner of a honey bottle, by getting into it. Can the owner solve the problem by making use of the notion of island constraint?

Unit 7

Negative-Constituent Preposing and SAI

Semantically negative constituents may be placed to the front of their sentences. The reason is that the speaker wants to emphasize the negative constituent. What is important to note is that the preposing of a negative constituent necessarily triggers Subject-Auxiliary Inversion (SAI). The following illustrate the rules:

(1) a. We may desert this city under no conditions.
b. *Under no conditions we may desert this city.
c. Under no conditions may we desert this city.

(2) a. I have never had to borrow money from the bank.
b. *Never I have had to borrow money from the bank.
c. Never have I had to borrow money from the bank.

(3) a. I saw nothing interesting on my tour to the country.
b. *Nothing interesting I saw on my tour to the country.
c. Nothing interesting did I see on my tour to the country.

(4) a. I go fishing only on Sunday.
b. *Only on Sunday I go fishing.
c. Only on Sunday do I go fishing.

(5) a. I eat such meat at no time.
b. *At no time I eat such meat.
c. At no time do I eat such meat.

In each of the (a) sentences, the underlined part is a negative constituent. One might wonder why *only on Sunday* and *at no time* are negative. One piece of evidence is this. When these are preposed, as in (b) and (c), the (c) versions are grammatical, while the (b) versions are not. The difference between the (b) versions and the (c) versions is whether the subjects and the auxiliaries are inverted or not. The grammaticality of the (c) versions in which the subject and the Aux are inverted and the ungrammaticality of the (b) versions in which the subject and the Aux are not inverted show that *only on Sunday* and *at no time* are negative. More concretely, *only* means *nothing but*. *At no time* means *never* because it means *not at any time*.

Consider the following examples:

(6) a. Not long ago there was a rainstorm.
b. *Not long ago was there a rainstorm.

(7) a. In no time at all they had routed the enemy.
b. *In no time at all had they routed the enemy.

(8) a. Not much later she arrived at the party.
b. *Not much later did she arrive at the party.

(9) a. With no help, she moved the piano upstairs.
b. *With no help did she move the piano upstairs.

(10) a. With no thought for his safety, he jumped into the river.
b. *With no thought for his safety did he jump into the river.

(11) a. With no hat on, he went out into the cold.
b. *With no hat on did he go out into the cold.

In each of the underlined parts above, there is a negative element. Hence, one might think that the underlined parts are negative constituents. Despite such expectations, the (b) versions in which the subjects and the auxiliaries are inverted are ungrammatical. Why is it? The reason is that the underlined parts have no negative meanings, which means that they are not negative constituents. This suggests that we must distinguish between "sentence-global negatives" and "local negatives". The former require SAI, while the latter do not. This distinction hinges on their meanings, but not their forms.

A relevant question is why sentence-global negatives necessarily trigger SAI, only when they are placed to the fronts of their sentences. Figuratively speaking, a serious national emergency surely requires its capital to move somewhere, while a local emergency does not require it to move.

I have mentioned, in the above, that whether a negative element makes a sentence-global negative constituent or a local negative constituent depends on its meaning. In this connection, there are cases in which a negative element may be ambiguous between a sentence-global negative and a local negative:

(12) a. For no reason, the teacher would beat his students.
b. For no reason would the teacher beat his students.

(13) a. For no money, she would dance naked.
b. For no money would she dance naked.

The same underlined parts are compatible with both the sentence-global negative sense and the local negative sense. This is due to the ambiguity of the underlined parts, which means that they have two different interpretations. Of course, the underlined parts have the sentence-global negative sense, when they occur with the SAI versions; otherwise, they have the local negative sense.

Seuren (1985:24) indicates that there is no SAI with *not only* in the front position when it modifies a definite subject term:

(14) a. Not only William sent his greetings.
b. *Not only did William send his greetings.

But there are such inversions when the subject is a quantified term:

(15) a. Not only did two friends of mine send their greetings.
b. *Not only two friends of mine sent their greetings.

(16) a. Not only did all of my friends send their greetings.
b. *Not only all of my friends sent their greetings.

This observation of Seuren's is quite interesting. But its explanation remains to be seen.

There is another interesting set of examples which involve embeddings:

(17) a. He believes that there are no such valuables in the box.
b. No such valuables does he believe that there are in the box.
c. **No such valuables he believes that are there in the box.
d. ?He believes that no such valuables are there in the box.

(18) a. He regrets that there are no such valuables in the box.
b. No such valuables does he regret that there are in the box.
c. **No such valuables he regrets that are there in the box.
d. ?He regrets that no such valuables are there in the box.

Since Postal (pc) gave me his grammatical judgments on these data, these judgments are very robust, except for the (d) examples, which seem somewhat strained for some unknown reasons, according to Postal. We can draw some generalizations from these data. First, when a negative constituent extracted from the complement is placed to the front of the whole sentence, SAI takes place in the main clause, but not in the complement. Second, when Negative-Constituent Preposing and SAI take place within the complement, the grammaticality of the whole sentence is marginal. To sum up, Negative-Constituent Preposing is not subject to the clause-mate condition, and the triggered SAI caused in the complement takes place in the main clause.

It is not the case that SAI is triggered only by Negative Constituent Preposing:

(19) a. If you should change your mind, I would also change mine.
b. Should you change your mind, I would also . . .

(20) a Even if you should change your mind, I would not change mine.
b. Should you change your mind, I would not . . .

The (a) versions may become the (b) versions, where SAI is involved. The expression *Should you change your mind* is ambiguous between condition (19a) and concession (20a). The content of the main clause disambiguates it. As *even if* suggests, the extreme point on the condition axis becomes concession (cf. Yang 1993g).

Exercises and problems

1. How do we know whether a negative element is sentence-global or local?
2. What is the semantic difference between a negative-constituent- preposed sentence and its source sentence?

3. Why is it that the sentence-global negative-constituent preposing triggers SAI, while the local negative-constituent preposing does not?
4. Does factivity (Kiparsky and Kiparsky 1970) affect Negative Constituent Preposing and its concomitant SAI?
5. Describe the difference of the following sentences with regard to Negative-Constituent Preposing and its concomitant SAI.
   a. *Only if/when* . . ., the main clause.
   b. The main clause, *only if/when* . . .
6. Provide evidence that *only* has some negative property.
7. Compare *at no time* and *in no time* with regard to negativity. These expressions are not idioms but "pseudo-idioms". Explain.
8. Translate sentences (12) and (13) into your mother tongue.
9. Explain Seuren's observation on examples (14–16).
10. Analyse the following sentence:

    On no one's account can logophoricity be defined in strictly syntactic terms.

11. Specify the rule involved in the following sentences:
    a. These two subjects, "I" and "you", occur more frequently with target verbs without "that" than do other subjects.
    b. "I" and "you" occur in target clauses without "that" more frequently than is the case of other subjects.

Unit 8

Metalinguistic Negation

One of the syntactically and semantically interesting topics is negation. It is usually claimed that negation may be studied from two different positions: ordinary negation and metalinguistic negation. Here we deal with metalinguistic negation. Ducrot (1972) defines metalinguistic negation: "a means for objection to a previous utterance on any grounds whatever" (cf. Horn 1985:134).

Metalinguistic negation has the following canonical structure, a three step structure:

(1) The structure of metalinguistic negation
  a. Trigger = previous utterance
  b. Rejoinder = metalinguistic negation = target-point negation = echo/ quotation rejoinder
  c. Correction/Rectification = follow-up sentence

Suppose a dialogue: (a) somebody utters an assertion, and then (b) somebody else rejoins the first speaker by negating, denying, objecting-to, rejecting, or opposing the previous utterance, and then (c) the same second speaker expresses his own (correct) opinion. This dialogue (discourse) structure matches (1), the structure of metalinguistic negation. The rejoinder may be echoing or non-echoing, but metalinguistic negation goes with only the echoing rejoinder.

The second speaker's rejoinder is expressed by negating a target-point of the trigger (= the previous utterance). In this sense, metalinguistic negation is "target-point negation." The target-point may be an overt element or a covert element. Overt elements include discourse, sentence, phrase, word, morpheme, spelling, tense, tone, sound, and the like. Covert elements include semantic feature, presupposition, implication, conversational implicature, and the like. The metalinguistic negation of this variety is possible by definition: "metalinguistic negation is a means for objecting to a previous utterance *on any grounds whatever*" (cf. Horn 1985:134; emphasis is mine).

Now illustration is in order. First I show metalinguistic negation of overt target-points (tri = trigger, rej = rejoinder, cor = correction):

(2) Discourse negation
  a. Tri: the previous discourse.
  b. Non-echo rej: I don't think so.
  c. Cor: the follow-up sentence.

(3) Sentence negation
  a. Tri: John is a philosopher.
  b. Echo rej: It is not the case that John is a philosopher.
  c. Cor: Smith was a linguist.

(4) Phrase negation
  a. Tri: John kissed Mary at a bus-stop.
  b. Rej: John did not kiss Mary at a bus-stop.
  c. Cor: John kissed Mary in a coffee shop.

(5) Word negation
  a. Tri: John studied at UCLA.
  b. Rej: John did not study at UCLA.
  c. Cor: John studied at UCL.

(6) Morpheme negation

a. Tri: John invited his advisor to the pulkoki party.
b. Rej: John did not invite his advisor to the pulkoki party.
c. Cor: John invited his advisee to the pulkoki party.

(7) Spelling negation
a. Tri: John is a humorer.
b. Rej: John is not a humorer.
c. Cor: John is a humorist.

(8) Tense negation
a. Tri: John is a chauvinist.
b. Rej: John is not a chauvinist.
c. Cor: John was a chauvinist.

(9) Tone negation
a. Tri: John pronounced "reMARKable".
b. Rej: John did not pronounce "reMARKable".
c. Cor: John pronounced "REmarkABLE".

(10) Sound negation
a. Tri: He is from [eimerikə].
b. Rej: He is not from [eimerikə].
c. Cor: He is from [əmerikə].

In the above examples (3) through (10), the underlined parts in the (a) sentences indicate the incorrectly uttered parts by the first speaker. The (b) sentences indicate the second speaker's objection to/denial/rejection/opposition of the previous utterance. The underlined parts in the (c) sentences indicate the corrections of the incorrectly uttered parts by the first speaker.

A serious question is why the correction/rectification sentence is necessary. Any rejoinder sentence (except tone and sound) in the above is ambiguous. Without the correction (= follow-up) sentence, the rejoinder sentence cannot be disambiguated, so that the second speaker's intention or message remains blurred. Hence, the correction sentence is indispensible in the frame of metalinguistic negation. Consider the following example:

(11) John did not kiss Mary at a bus-stop. (= 4b)

This negative sentence is multiply ambiguous because the negatable target points and their combinations are multiple. The negatable target-points are: *John*, *Mary*, *bus-stop*, *kiss*, *tense*, and their combinations. This means that the second speaker's rejoinder sentence (= the metalinguistic negation sentence) is multiply ambiguous. Although the second speaker does not want to invite ambiguity, the form of the rejoinder negative sentence cannot get rid of it. Hence, the same second speaker is forced to disambiguate the ambiguous rejoinder sentence, by means of the correction (= follow-up) sentence. It should be noted that the rejoinder negative sentence, in which tone or sound is negated, is not ambiguous, because the negation's target point is clearly marked.

Covert elements may also become target-points of negation:

(12) Semantic feature

a. Tri: Harry killed the politician.

b. Rej: Harry did neither kill nor murder the politician.

c. Cor: Harry assassinated the politician.

In (12), *kill* may be accidental or intentional, *murder* is intentional, while *assassinate* is intentional and the object noun must be a politician. Thus, in (12b), which expresses metalinguistic negation, what is negated/objected to/denied/rejected is neither *kill* nor *murder*, but the semantic feature which distinguishes between *kill/murder* and *assassinate*.

Now consider the following:

(13) Presupposition
   a. Tri: The king of France is bald.
   b. Rej: The king of France is not bald.
   c. Cor: France does not have a king.

When a speaker utters (13a), he presupposes that France has a king by the expression of *the king of France*. In (13b), metalinguistic negation, what is negated/ rejected/objected to/denied may be the king's being bald if there is a king in France. But, in fact, there is no king in France. Hence, what is negated cannot be the king's being bald. Then, what is negated in (13b)? What is negated is the presupposition that there is a king in France, which is confirmed by the follow-up sentence (13c). In zero context, (13b) is multiply ambiguous:

(14) The king of France is not bald. (= 13b)
   a. The Prime Minister of France is bald.
   b. The king of England is bald.
   c. The Prime Minister of Canada is bald.
   d. The king of France was bald.
   e. There is no king of France.
   etc.

This multiple ambiguity is due to the existence of some target-points of negation. But in the context of (13), what is negated is the presupposition (= 14e).

Next, consider the following:

(15) Implication
   a. Tri: John managed to open the door.
   b. Rej: John did not manage to open the door.
   c. Cor: The door opens easily.

(15a) implies that the door was not easy to open. This implication is negated in (15b), a metalinguistically negative sentence, which is confirmed by (15c). Here also, (15b), a rejoinder negative sentence (= metalinguistically negative sentence), is multiply ambiguous, which is disambiguated by (15c). This shows that implication can also be a target-point of negation.

Conversational implicature may also be a target-point of negation. In the case of implication, a sentence implies another sentence. In the case of implicature, in contrast, the speaker implicates another sentence by uttering a sentence:

(16) <u>Conversational implicature</u>

a. Tri: The milkman has come.

b. Rej: The milkman has not yet come. Let me sleep a little more.

c. Cor: It's still 4.

In (16a), what is conversationally implicated is: it is 5 or 6 o'clock. In (16b), what is negated is the conversational implicature made in (16a), which is confirmed by (16c).

Through examples (14–16), I have shown that any covert element can also be metalinguistically negated. Except for morphological negatives, the negation of any type is forced to be expressed in the form of "sentence negation", by which I mean that "negation is expressed in a sentence form". This formal restriction for the expression of negation is the unique source of ambiguity, because there are multiple target-points of negation. For this reason, I claim that "metalinguistic negation is the target-point negation".

In Yang (1993c), I suggested "scale-point negation" for the account of scalar examples:

(17) a. Sue is happy.
b. Sue is not happy, Sue is ecstatic.

(18) a. Sue is miserable.
b. Sue is not miserable, Sue is sad.

In (17b), if what is negated is the property of being happy, the whole sentence is contradictory. Nevertheless, it is not contradictory, because negation negates the scale point of *happy* out of the scale points of *miserable - sad - happy - ecstatic*. (18b) is understood in the same frame. What I want to claim is that scale-point negation can be incorporated into target-point negation, which is metalinguistic negation. (17) and (18) can be rephrased in the frame of metalinguistic negation:

(17') a. Tri: Sue is happy.
b. Rej: Sue is not happy.
c. Cor: Sue is ecstatic (or sad, or miserable).

(18') a. Tri: Sue is miserable.
b. Rej: Sue is not miserable.
c. Cor: Sue is sad (or happy, or ecstatic).

Notice that the correction sentences in (17') and (18') are not confined to any specific ones. This is due to the nature of target points available in the negative rejoinder sentences. It should be indicated that the morphological negatives *un-* and *in-* cannot function as rejoinders because they do not cause ambiguous target points.

Note that the three step structure of metalinguistic negation can be reduced to two steps, by collapsing the rejoinder sentence and the correction sentence. This collapsing is natural since the rejoinder sentence and the correction sentence are uttered by the same second speaker. For example,

(19) a. Tri: Bill is a philosopher.
b/c. Rej/Cor: Bill is not a philosopher but a linguist.
(or): Bill is a linguist, but not a philosopher.

Finally, a serious question is: if metalinguistic negation can be properly expressed by the two step structure, what is the real difference between "metalinguistic negation" and "ordinary negation"? I don't see any significant difference, although the current literature emphasize the difference.

Exercises and problems

1. Can "scale-point negation" be incorporated into "target-point negation", which is metalinguistic negation?
2. Can negation negate any aspect of a sentence? How?
3. What is the definition of metalinguistic negation?
4. What is the difference between "ordinary negation" and "metalinguistic negation"? Can they be collapsed?
5. Why is it that a sentence becomes multiply ambiguous when it is negated?
6. What is the function of the correction (- follow up) sentence?
7. What is the difference of morphological and syntactic negatives?
8. Explain metalinguistic negation involved in the following:

   A: You look healthy.

   B: I don't look healthy. I am healthy.

Unit 9

Clefting and Pseudo-Clefting

Clefting

A certain element can be picked up from a sentence, and be placed in the focus position: [*It is* [focus position] *that/who* ⋯]. The clefted elements are focused. They are "focus elements". I refer to [*It be* [focus position]] and [*that/who*⋯] as "focus clause" and "home clause", respectively. This rule is called "Clefting" or "Cleft Extraposition". The following illustrate the rule:

(1) a. A tax break was counted on.
  b. It was <u>a tax break</u> that was counted on.

(2) a. I am enjoying reading Yang's humor book.
  b. It is <u>reading Yang's humor book</u> that I am enjoying.

(3) a. Kim spoke to Susan in "Worldish".
  b. It was <u>to Susan</u> that Kim spoke in "Worldish".

In the above examples, the underlined parts are clefted elements. Categorially, cleftable (= focus) elements include NP, Gerund, PP, Adverbs of some types. We will see below that other categories can also be clefted.

Consider the following examples:

(4) a. I didn't go mountain climbing because it was snowing.
  b. It was <u>because it was snowing</u> that I didn't go mountain climbing.

(5) a. Bolinger produced more books and articles after he was retired.
b. It was after he was retired that Bolinger produced more books and articles.

(6) a. Sue had a son before she was married.
b. It was before she was married that Sue had a son.

(7) a. Kim has been confident of independent research since he got a Ph.D.
b. It was since he got a Ph.D. that Kim has been confident of independent research.

(8) a. Joan began to wear a strange dress in order to attract boy students' attention.
b. It was (in order) to attract boy students' attention that Joan began to wear a strange dress.

As seen in the above examples, the cleftable elements also include *because*-clause, *after*-clause, *before*-clause, temporal *since*-clause, and *in-order-to*-clause (= infinitival complement of purpose use).

Reason clauses include *because*-clause, *as*-clause, *for*-clause, and *since*-clause. Curiously enough, only *because*-clause is cleftable out of the reason clauses. Is this accidental? There must be some reason. The most plausible reason is this: the cleftability requires some strong reason. This is the reason why only *because*-clause can be clefted. It expresses the strongest reason, as compared with other reason clauses. This strong-vs-weak hypothesis seems to be supported by the following examples (Postal 1994:178):

(9) a. *It was it that they believed/discussed/denied.
b. It was that that they believed/discussed/denied.

The difference of these sentences comes from the difference of *it* vs. *that*. The former is weak, and the latter is strong. If (9b) is grammatical, the underlined *that* must get a strong stress, so that it can be distinguished from the next *that*, which is the sentential complementizer.

Interestingly enough, the difference between *because* and the others (*for, since, as*) is also reflected in some other constructions (cf. Grosu 1972):

(10) The chopping of elements of the main clause
  a. Who did John jilt because she had no money?
  b. *Who did John jilt {as, for, since} she had no money?

(11) The occurrence in embedded clauses
  a. I believe [John left the country because he was unhappy].
  b. *I believe [John left the country {as, since, for} he was unhappy].

(12) Ambiguity with negation
  a. He doesn't beat his wife because he loves her.
  b. He doesn't beat his wife {as, since, for} he loves her.

As well known, Lakoff's classical example (12a) is ambiguous. But if *because* is replaced by other reason words, sentence (12b) is not ambiguous, unlike (12a).

Consider the following examples:

(13) a. The professor emeritus realizes that his status is not regarded as an honorable one.
  b. *It is that his status is not regarded as an honorable one that the professor emeritus realizes.
  c. It is the fact that his status is not regarded as an honorable one that the professor emeritus realizes.

(13b) shows that the sentential complement cannot be clefted. In contrast, (13c) shows that the head noun plus content clause can be clefted. That is, if a sentential complement has a head noun (= head noun + content clause), it can be clefted. The underlined part in (13c) is a complex NP, which is categorially an NP, which is cleftable. This is the difference between (13b) and (13c). A complex NP has two sources: one is the NP followed by a relative clause, and the other is the NP followed by a content clause (cf. Yang 1993d). (Content clauses and relative clauses will be dealt with in Unit 11.)

Emonds (1972:41–44) claims that gerunds (of one type) are NPs, but infinitival complements are not:

(14) a. For John to drive carelessly upsets me.
b. *It's for John to drive carelessly that upsets me.

(15) a. John's driving carelessly upsets me.
b. It's John's driving carelessly that upsets me.

(14b) shows that an infinitival complement cannot be placed in the focus position. One might see that (14b) conflicts with (8b). The clefted/focused infinitival complement in (8b) does not have a subject, while the clefted/focused infinitival complement in (14b) has a subject. However, this is not a conflict, because the infinitival complement in (14b) does not express any purpose while the infinitive in (8b) expresses purpose. That is, the infinitival complement of purpose use can occur in the focus position. (15b) shows that gerundival complements can be placed in the focus position. Emonds indicates that one type of gerunds can be clefted. This implies that other type(s) of gerunds cannot be clefted. He provides the following examples:

(16) a. *It is playing for some time that they are doing.
b. *It was drinking beer from the bottle that she kept.
c. *It was stealing my money that she caught him.

He provides these examples just to show that another type of gerunds is not cleftable. These data call for some explanation. My wild speculation is this: the main verbs and the clefted gerunds have some sort of close links, so that they are hardly separated.

The most difficult problem in Clefting is whether adjectives and adverbs can occur in the cleft focus position. References on this matter are not available. I posit the following hypothesis:

(17) Hypothesis for Adjective's/Adverb's occurrability in cleft focus position

If an adjective/adverb cannot meet the following conditions, it cannot occur in the cleft focus position.

a. separability condition in the home clause
b. compatibility condition in the focus clause

If the home clause makes sense even without an adjective/adverb, the adjective/adverb meets the separability condition. If an adjective/adverb is compatible with copula *be* or its equivalent, it meets the compatibility condition. This hypothesis will be validated below.

Adverbs of most sub-types may occur in the cleft focus position:

(18) a. Questions of this sort could be seriously posed recently.
b. It is recently that questions of this sort could be seriously posed. (time)

(19) a. Kim keeps money in the jar, not in the safe.
b. It is in the jar, not in the safe that Kim keeps money. (place)

(20) a. The swindler was beaten with a stick.
b. It was with a stick that the swindler was beaten. (instrument)

(21) a. He was killed by a terrorist.
b. It was by a terrorist that he was killed. (agent)

Normally, manner adverbs cannot occur in the focus position:

(22) a. John argued against Harry explicitly.
b. *It was explicitly that John argues against Harry.

(23) a. John examined the document carefully.
b. *It was carefully that John examined the document.

(24) a. Susan dances elegantly.
b. *It is elegantly that Susan dances.

(25) a. They cook in the French style.
b. ?It is in the French style that they cook.

Thus, adverbs are divided into manner adverbs and others, with respect to their occurrability in the focus position. The reason why manner adverbs cannot occur in the focus position is that they cannot meet the compatibility condition although they meet the separability condition. Manner adverbs require action/activity verbs, and copula is not compatible with manner adverbs. Hence, manner adverbs cannot occur in the focus position. Other adverbs meet the two conditions, and they can occur in the focus position.

Quirk *et al* (1985:561) indicate that manner adverbs cannot be the focus of a cleft sentence, but their acceptability is increased if they are modified or if the focus clause is interrogated or negated:

(26) a. *It was carefully that John examined the document.
b. ?Was it carefully that John examined the document?

(27) a. ?It's in the French style that they cook.
b. It isn't in the French style that they cook.

(28) a. ??It was violently/loudly that they argued.
b. (?)It was so very violently/loudly that they argued.

The (b) versions in (26–28) are relatively better than the (a) versions. An interesting question is: why is it that the (b) versions are better? I think it is not accidental. If the focus clause is modified/emphasized, interrogated or negated, it carries relatively stronger information. This accords with the function of the focus clause, which was already mentioned in the above.

Normally, adjectives cannot occur in the focus position:

(29) a. Susan is happy.
b. *It is happy that Susan is.

Thus, one might generalize focus elements as: NPs can occur in the cleft focus position, whereas adjectives cannot. This categorial generalization, however, is too strong. Interestingly enough, there are opposite cases: NPs cannot occur in the focus position, whereas adjectives can:

(30) a. He was the chairman.
b. ?The chairman he was. (Collins's (1991) (28a))
c. The chairman was he.
d. ?It was the chairman that he was. (Collins's (1991) (28b))

(31) a. He painted the house green.
b. It was green that he painted the house. (Collins's (1991) (16))

Examples (30d) and (31b) are counterexamples to the generalization made above.

These counterexamples are not accidental. In the case of NPs (30), an NP of the predicate-nominal (i.e. subj + *be* + noun) cannot be topicalized (cf. (30b)), nor can be clefted (cf. (30d)), although it can be involved in Subject-Verb Inversion (cf. (30c)). The ungrammaticality (marginality, at best) of (30b) and (30d) is due to the fact that NPs are reluctant to be separated from copula *be*, just like adjectives (already indicated in the above). This means that the string of "*be* + NP/Adj" is a coherent unit.

In the case of adjectives, they must be distinguished, in terms of their functions, between "predicate adjectives" (i.e. subj + *be* + adj) and "adjunct adjectives" (i.e. ··· object + adj). Sentence (31b) shows that "adjunct adjectives" can occur in the cleft focus position, unlike "predicate adjectives". This distinction of adjectives is not accidental. Predicate adjectives cannot meet the separability condition although they meet the compatibility condition. Hence, they cannot occur in the focus position. In contrast, adjunct adjectives meet the two conditions. Hence, they can occur in the focus position. This shows that the hypothesis in (17) is validated.

"Adjunct adjectives" must be further specified. The acceptability contrast of (32b) and (33b) below (from Borkin 1984) might challenge "adjunct adjectives":

(32) a. They painted it scarlet.
b. (?)It was scarlet that they painted it. (Borkin's (1984) (36b))
c. *They painted it scarletly.

(33) a. They hammered it flat.
b. *It was flat that they hammered it. (Borkin's (1984) (36a))
c. They hammered it flatly.

Although both *scarlet* and *flat* function as adjunct adjectives in the source sentences (32a, 33a), *flat* does not behave like an adjunct adjective in the cleft sentence (33b). This is not groundless. *Flat* in (33a, b) is not a pure adjective but a "manner-adverbial adjective". What I call "manner-adverbial adjectives" refer to adjectives which replace manner adverbs. That is, *flat* in (33a) has replaced *flatly* in (33c). This view is supported by the song-title of *Love me tender*, which replaces *Love me tenderly* for some rhythmical reason. In (32), in contrast, *scarlet* does not replace **scarletly* (cf. 32a vs. 32c). Thus, "manner-adverbial adjectives", which may function as adjuncts, must be distinguished from "adjunct adjectives". Recall that manner adverbs cannot occur in the cleft focus position, which was mentioned above. Likewise, manner-adverbial adjectives cannot occur in the cleft focus position.

Borkin (1984:136–137), following Bolinger (1972), attempts to explain examples (32b) and (33b) in terms of "referentiality". She argues that, since the subject "*it*" of the cleft sentence is "referential", the element in the focus position must also be "referential". However, she herself admits that "referentiality" has the problem of "total accountability", which is clearly mentioned in the following (Borkin 1984:137):

> [I]t can be seen that referentiality, or the plausibility of referentiality, is important for the acceptability of particular constituents in focus position. I do not mean to imply that it is the only consideration, however; it is much less clear, for example, how all of the . . . differences in acceptability [shown in her examples (37)-(40)] are related to referentiality, and I will not argue that they are.

The expression, copula *be* or "its equivalent" (= *be*'s equivalent), is explicated below:

(34) a. John looks happy.
b. *It is happy that John looks.

(35) a. The food tastes delicious.
b. *It is delicious that the food tastes.

The ungrammaticality of the (b) versions can be explained by "*be*'s equivalent". *Be*'s equivalent in (34) is *look*, and *be*'s equivalent in (35) is *taste*. Thus, *be*'s equivalents refer to intransitive verbs followed by NP/ Adjective. (*Become* seems to be exceptional (cf. Quirk *et al* 1985:1385).)

The coherent unit of "*be* + NP/Adj" must be extended to PP:

(36) a. Mary put the apples on the table.
b. It was on the table that Mary put the apples.

(37) a. The apples were on the table.
b. *It was on the table that the apples were.

The grammaticality contrast of (36b) and (37b) shows that the string of "*be* + PP" behaves like "*be* + NP/Adj" in connection with some element's occurrability in the cleft focus position. It should be noted that adjective's occurrability in the cleft focus position seems to be subject to idiolectal variation.

Consider the following conjunctions:

(38) a. They need (both) wealth and health.
b. It is <u>(both) wealth and health</u> that they need.

(39) a. They need health as well as wealth.
b. It is <u>health as well as wealth</u> that they need.

(40) a. They need not only wealth but also health.
b. It is <u>not only wealth but also health</u> that they need.

(41) a. They need health in addition to wealth.
b. It is health in addition to wealth that they need.

As expected, the underlined conjuncts can be placed in the focus position. What is curious is the *let alone* conjunction:

(42) a. They need health, let alone wealth.
b. *It is health, let alone wealth that they need.

Coordinate conjunctions (38–41) and the *let alone* conjunction (42) look rather similar. But, as shown in (42), the *let alone* conjunction cannot be placed in the cleft focus position. Syntactically, the difference between proper coordinate conjunctions and the *let alone* conjunction is reflected not only in Clefting but also in Topicalization, WH-extraction and VP-Deletion. For details, see Fillmore *et al* (1988:515–516).

I indicated, in the above, that NPs can occur in the focus position. This generalization, however, must be a little bit weakened, because there are cases where indirect objects (IOs) cannot occur in the focus position:

(43) a. John gave Mary a book.
b. It was a book that John gave Mary.
c. *It was Mary that John gave a book.
d. It was to Mary that John gave a book.
e. It was Mary that John gave a book to.
f. *It was Mary a book that John gave.
g. *It was a book to Mary that John gave.

(44) a. John bought Mary a book.
b. It was a book that John bought Mary.
c. *It was Mary that John bought a book.
d. It was for Mary that John bought a book.

e. It was Mary that John bought a book for.
f. *It was Mary a book that John bought.
g. *It was a book for Mary that John bought.

The (c, f, g) versions show that IOs cannot occur in the focus position, together with or without DOs. The (d, e) versions show that Dative-shifted IOs can occur in the focus position, with or without Preposition-stranded. Interestingly enough, this is not an isolated behavior of Clefting; some speakers do not allow IOs to be extracted, regardless of extraction constructions (cf. Unit 17).

Exercises and problems

1. What categories can or cannot be placed in the cleft focus position? How about adjectives?
2. Why is it that the *because*-clause behaves differently from other reason clauses, with respect to Clefting?
3. Why is it that the *since*-clause can or cannot be clefted?
4. A sentential complement cannot be placed in the cleft focus position. How can we make it grammatical?
5. What type of the infinitival complement can be placed in the focus position?
6. Can the gerundival complement be placed in the focus position?
7. What types of adverbs and adjectives can be placed in the focus position?
8. Specify the condition under which NPs, adjectives and PPs cannot occur in the cleft focus position.

9. What is the difference of the following?
    a. It was Bill that didn't come to the party.
    b. It wasn't Bill that came to the party.
10. Explain the following data:
    (1) a. They launched an attack against the city.
        b. It was against the city that they launched an attack.
    (2) a. They watched an attack against the city.
        b. *It was against the city that they watched an attack.

Pseudo-Clefting

Now Pseudo-clefting is in order. This rule is also known as WH-cleft. Emonds (1972:54) indicates that categories such as NP, AP, PP, VP, S can appear in the pseudo-cleft focus position:

(45) a. What I dislike is a coward. (NP)
     b. What John is is very brave. (AP)
     c. Where he rolled was down the hill. (PP)
     d. What we should do is keep peace on the earth. (VP)
     e. What they don't realize is that we must support scientists. (Sentential Complement)
     f. What he wants is finding out the hard-to-find books. (Gerundival Complement)

In these examples, the underlined parts show that the categories indicated above can occur in the pseudo-cleft focus position (= the position where the underlined part occur). The above examples do not include infinitival complement, which will be discussed later.

One important point to be confirmed is whether all WH-words can occur in the initial position:

(46) a. Who I admire most is the inventor of electricity.
b. What I need is social recognition.
c. Where I met my wife first was in an "ice-cake" shop.
d. When I met her first was in 1960.
e. Why I met her first was to marry.
f. How I met her first was via the match-maker.

These examples show that any WH-word can occur in the initial position. That is my wish. What is true is that WH-words except *what* depend on dialects/idiolects. The relevant noun may precede the WH-word except *what*: *the one who . . ., the place where . . ., the time when . . ., the reason why . . ., the way how . . . .* The reason that a noun cannot precede *what* is this: the noun *the thing* is already lexically incorporated in *what*: *the thing which → what.*

Pseudo-cleft/WH-cleft constructions may be inverted:

(47) a. What we did was that we built an igloo.
b. We built an igloo was what we did.

(48) a. What we did was interview the applicants.
b. Interview the applicants was what we did.

This invertability also depends on dialects/idiolects.

In (45), infinitival complement was not illustrated. The following, from Emonds (1972:54), illustrate infinitival complement:

(49) a. For Mary to be late upsets me.
b. What upsets me is <u>for Mary to be late</u>.

However, whether infinitival complements can occur in the pseudo-cleft focus position is controversial:

Rosenbaum (1967:77) is negative:

(50) *What happened was <u>for John to find gold</u>.

Baker (1978:145–6) is affirmative:

(51) What Sharon wanted was <u>for everyone to keep silent</u>.

Akmajian & Heny (1975:317) are affirmative:

(52) What I would prefer is <u>for you to get out of here</u>.

Postal (1974:132) is negative on the bare subject infinitival complement, but affirmative on the subjectless one:

(53) a. *What Joan found was <u>Barbara to be pregnant</u>.
b. What I want is <u>to become a millionaire</u>.

As seen in the above, the eminent scholars' grammatical judgments are divided, with regard to the infinitival complement in the pseudo-cleft focus position. This suggests that it depends on dialects/idiolects.

For some semantic, functional, and discourse aspects of the cleft and pseudo-cleft constructions, see Borkin (1984) and Collins (1991).

Exercises and problems

1. What WH-words can occur in the initial position of pseudo-cleft constructions?
2. Compare Clefting and Pseudo-clefting in terms of focus.
3. Can the verb *force* be used in the pre-*be* part?
4. Why is it that stative verbs like *like* cannot be placed in the pseudo-cleft focus position? (cf. Emonds 1972:54–57)

   *What John did was (to) *like* potatoes.
5. Compare the structures of the following sentences:

   a. What I want is to help my students.

   b. What I want is help my students.
6. What is the structural difference of the following?

   a. What is strange is that he never exchanges greetings with others.

   b. Strange is that he never exchanges greetings . . .
7. Explain the following data:

   (1) a. John seems to know the answer.

   b. *What John seems is to know the answer.

   (2) a. John wants to know the answer.

   b. What John wants is to know the answer.

Unit 10

VP Preposing

A significant question is: why does the speaker prepose an element out of a sentence? The natural answer is: the speaker wants to make the element "outstanding". That is, the preposed element is "emphasized". This property is common in all preposing rules. VP Preposing is not an exception. In a discourse, for instance, the second speaker may want to affirm or suspend the first speaker's "salient proposition". The second speaker's intention of this is expressed by VP Preposing since the VP is the most representative part of a proposition.

Consider the following discourse part:

(1) Speaker A: . . . John passed the exam . . .
Speaker B: Bill says that John passed the exam.

(2) Speaker A: . . . John passed the exam . . .
Speaker B: Bill says that John passed the exam, and <u>pass the exam</u> he did.

In (1), the second speaker just repeats part of what the first speaker said. In (2), in contrast, the second speaker not only repeats part of what the first speaker said, but also emphasizes the predication part of the repeated proposition. In the process of emphasizing, he/she preposes the VP, the underlined part of (2b). This preposing is called VP Preposing.

Suppose a speaker said the following:

(3) #John passed the exam, and pass the exam he did.

In (3), the second conjunct (i.e. the follow-up sentence) has VP Preposing, but information-wise, it signifies nothing. Hence, sentence (3) is an example of "discourse infelicity" (marked by #). That is, (3) is not an example of VP Preposing.

Ward (1990) argues that VP Preposing has two discourse functions: proposition affirmation and proposition suspension. They are defined as follows. The former is to affirm a speaker's belief in a salient proposition explicitly evoked in the prior discourse. The latter is to suspend a speaker's belief in a salient proposition explicitly evoked in the prior discourse. That is, to suspend (i.e. weaken) the salient proposition by conditionalizing the logically dependent (i.e. entailed, or presupposed) proposition.

The following illustrate the proposition affirmation of VP Preposing:

(4) a. Mary once predicted that scientists can clone animals, and clone animals they now have.
b. John intends to meet the Pope, and meet the Pope he will.
c. The old woman has never bought a car, and buy one she never will.
d. They hoped that Koreans would unify the country, but unify it they have not yet.

The underlined parts illustrate VP Preposing, which affirms the speaker's belief in the salient proposition.

The following, in contrast, illustrate proposition suspension:

(5) a. Mary finished her thesis late, if finish it she did.
b. It is strange that John objected to the proposal, if object to it he did.

c. It is shocking that she killed her baby, if kill it she did.
d. John drinks only "soju", if drink it he does.

In these sentences, the preposed VPs are conditionalized, which means that the proposition is suspended.

I would like to refer readers to Ward (1990) for discourse functions of VP Preposing. From now on, I will discuss formal aspects of the rule. Compare the following examples:

(6) a. John passed the exam, and pass the exam he did.
b. *John passed the exam, and passed the exam he does.
c. *John passed the exam, and passed the exam he.

In (6), the grammaticality hinges on the structure of the VP-preposed sentence. This means that the rule under consideration requires some specific formal restrictions. In each of the second sentences in (6), the VP is preposed. Nonetheless, only the first example is grammatical; the other two are ungrammatical, which is due to the failure of the rule's formal requirement. Intuitively, the starred forms look like the forms produced by the rule. But this intuition fails.

Notice that the verb of the VP-preposed part in (6a) has the stem form, whereas the verbs in (6b, c) have the tensed forms. This difference is the very point at issue. The rule must have the following structure:

(7) Structure of VP Preposing
a. 1st sentence + conjunction + VP-preposed sentence
b. conjunction: *and, but, if*
c. VP-preposed S: verb stem + (object) + subject + Aux
d. Aux: modal Aux, *have, be, do*

The choice of conjunction depends on the discourse function. The preposed verb must take the "stem form". This formal requirement is not satisfied in (6b). And this requirement is the reason why the rule under consideration is referred to as "VP" Preposing. Technically, VP necessarily takes the verb stem, which may be transformed by being combined with Aux (cf. Yang 1993a). The ungrammaticality of (6c) is due to the lack of Aux, and the non-stem form of the verb.

The "VP" in VP-Preposing refers to the "VP" of Chomsky's (1965) Aspects-model. Therein, PS rules start with "S --> NP - Aux - VP". The "verb" in "VP" refers to the verb stem. The verb stems get relevant affixes by Affix-Hopping. This clarification of "VP" will remove our curiosity about the starred examples in the following:

(8) a. *They say John passed the exam, and passed the exam he does.
    b. ························, and pass the exam he did.

(9) a. *They say John has passed the exam, and passed the exam he has.
    b. ····························, and pass the exam he has.

(10) a. They predict John will pass the exam, and pass the exam he will.
     b. They predict John can pass the exam, and pass the exam he can.

The contrast of (a) and (b) in (8) and (9) is the contrast of the stem form and the non stem form of the preposed verb.

Another formal requirement is the "explicitness" condition. Ward indicates that the preposed VP requires the existence of the corresponding lexically explicit counterpart in the main sentence. Otherwise, the VP-preposed sentence is not grammatical:

(11) a. Betty wasn't hungry. But she ate.
     b. *Betty wasn't hungry, but eat she did.

(12) a. He told his boss he was going to quit. And he resigned.
b. *He told his boss he was going to quit, and resign he did.

(13) a. The student didn't mean to insult his teacher. But he upset him.
b. *The student didn't mean to insult his teacher, but upset him he did.

(14) a. Inside the Coors truck was beer for the students' consumption. And they drank.
b. *Inside the Coors truck was beer for the stuedents' consumption, and drink they did.

(15) a. Tchaikovski was one of the most tormented men in musical history. But he produced music.
b. *Tchaikovski was one of the most tormented men in musical history, but produce music he did.

In each of the (b) sentences, the underlined verbs share some semantic feature, but it is not grammatical, because the explicitness condition is not satisfied. In (15b), the underlined verb has no counterpart whatsoever in the main sentence. In cases like this, the VP-preposed sentences are not allowed; instead, the (a) versions are used. Thus, the "explicitness" condition is better expressed as the "echo" condition (cf. Yang 1993a).

In the case of word order, specifically the order of direct object and indirect object of dative sentences, my test of the explicitness condition through informants shows that the explicitness condition depends on dialects/ idiolects. Some other tests result in the similar way (cf. Yang 1993a).

There are some rules similar to VP Preposing:

(16) a. Relativization (cf. Thompson 1971:88–89)
I proposed that I will wash the dishes, which I will.

b. Resumptive Clause Topicalization (cf. Haiman 1985:55)
He sat down. Having sat down, he undid his tie.

c. *So*-Preposing
I said that I will wash the dishes, and so I will.

d. VP-Preposing
I said that I will wash the dishes, and wash the dishes I will.

The underlined parts above share something like VP-Preposing. Among them, *So*-Preposing and VP-Preposing are most similar. Structurally, *So*-Preposing can replace VP-Preposing, but not vice versa, since *so* can cover wider material than VP can do. For instance, *so* can replace what I call VAR (verb and the rest), but VP cannot. If what has been called VP of VP-Preposing must be replaced by VAR, the two rules can be converted. Nonetheless, such a conversion is not allowed, because they are not the same in meaning and use: *So*-Preposing is used when the speaker agrees with the salient proposition of the prior discourse, whereas VP-Preposing is used when the speaker independently verifies the salient proposition (William O'Grady p.c.). This difference is supported by Joseph E. Emonds (p.c.), who says that *So*-Preposing emphasizes truth, and VP-Preposing emphasizes content of VP.

Now consider the following examples:

(17) a. They say that John is a genius, and a genius he is.
b. It is said that dogs are quite intelligent, and intelligent they are.

In (17), the preposed elements are NP in (a) and Adjective in (b). Hence, we can say that these sentences include NP-Preposing and Adj-Preposing. Ward (1990) separates these from VP-Preposing. However, these rules must be subsumed under VP-Preposing because adjectives and predicate-nominals are VPs (cf. Yang 1993a).

The final question here is whether the preposable elements in VP Preposing are confined only to VP or go beyond it:

(18) It is said that Sue criticized Bill for the matter without any evidence, and criticize Bill for the matter <u>without any evidence</u> she did.

In (18), the underlined part is not inside VP (cf. Unit 28). This single example seems to be sufficient to claim that what is preposable is VAR (= verb and the rest), which subsumes VP (cf. Yang 1993a:21).

Exercises and problems

1. Describe the difference of VP-Preposing and *So*-Preposing.
2. What rules are similar to VP-Preposing?
3. Can what is preposable go beyond VP?
4. Specify the explicitness condition, and discuss whether this condition is sufficient.
5. Is the explicitness condition a syntactic requirement or a semantic requirement?
6. In the following sentence, is VP-Preposing involved? If yes, describe how it is involved.

   Susan dances well, and which I don't.

Unit 11

Content Clauses vs. Relative Clauses

The relative clause and the content clause look almost similar. Both have the head noun which is followed by a clause/sentence. However, they are quite different both in structure and in meaning. In the case of relative clauses, the relative clause "modifies" the head noun. In the case of content clauses, in contrast, the content clause "specifies" the head noun. The contrast of "modification" and "specification" is one of the characteristics for distinguishing the two constructions.

They have the following canonical forms:

(1) a. Relative clause: head noun - pronoun - sentence
    b. Content clause: head noun - *that* - sentence

Since one of the pronouns in the relative clause is *that*, the two constructions look the same if the pronoun is *that*. But they are different in structure:

(2) a. Relative clause: the fact that John knows [e].
    b. Content clause: the fact that John knows Korean.

The two structures in (2) have the same head noun and the same connector. But in (2a), the verb lacks its object in its clause, while the verb in (2b) has its object. This is the essential difference of the two structures.

In a nutshell, if some element is missing in the clause which follows the connector, the missed element refers to the head noun: this is the case of relative clauses. In contrast, if something is not missing in the following clause, this clause is the content clause. In other words, if the head noun is identical to the missing element, the clause is a relative clause. In contrast, if the head noun has no missing element in the clause, the clause is a content clause. Thus, the difference is the presence or the absence of the missing element in the following clause. (2a) is an example of relative clause. Here the relative clause "modifies" the head noun. (2b) is an example of content clause. Here the content clause "specifies" the head noun. Out of context, we don't know what *the fact* means in (2b). The head noun *fact* is vague: this shortage of information is filled with the content clause. The meaning of "content clause" is the content of the head noun. This is not the case with relative clauses.

Since relative clauses are well known, I would like to concentrate on the content clause. In terms of form, the content clause is equivalent to the sentential complement, and the connector *that* is equivalent to the sentential complementizer. In terms of function, the content clause "specifies" the head noun. In the process of the explication of the content clause, the differences of the two constructions will clearly be closed up.

Consider the following examples:

(3) a. We believe Paul's claim that the country initiated the attack against its neighbor country.

b. Jim raises (against Paul) the objection that the country did not initiate the attack against its neighbor country.

c. Tom supports Jim's denial that the country initiated the attack against its neighbor country.

The underlined nouns are head nouns for the following content clauses. Suppose these sentences are sequentially uttered. What attracts our attention is that the head nouns in these sentences have different semantic functions. In (3a), the content clause describes the head noun *claim*. In (3c), in contrast, the head noun *denial* negates the content clause: that is, Jim's position is that the country did not initiate the attack. Hence, the head noun *claim* is affirmative, and the head noun *denial* is negative. This distinction is not accidental; the head nouns and their content clauses have the following relations:

(4) a. Paul claims that the country initiated the attack. (cf. 3a)
b. Jim denies that the country initiated the attack. (cf. 3c)

On this basis, I (Yang 1993d) argue that the head nouns must be distinguished into (i) affirmative head nouns and (ii) negative head nouns. The latter include *denial, doubt, misconception,* etc.

What is interesting is sentence (3b), where the head noun *objection* is involved. If asked about *objection*, non-native speakers of English usually regard this head noun as a negative one. To put the conclusion first, however, the judgment is the misunderstanding of the words, *object, object to,* and *objection*:

(5) a. Jim objects that the country initiated the attack.
b. Jim objects to it that the country initiated the attack.

In (5a), what Jim opposes is not the content/meaning of the content clause, but Paul's claim, for example in (3b). This means that Jim opposes Paul's claim by means of the meaning/message of the content clause. In (5b), in contrast, Jim opposes the meaning of the content clause. In short, the verb *object* is not negative while the verb *object to* is negative. Thus, I (Yang 1993d) categorize the head nouns, *objection*, *rebuttal*, etc. as pseudo-negative head nouns, which look negative, but are affirmative. In (5b), the pronoun *it* is required because the preposition *to* cannot occur with a sentential complement.

What should be considered at this point is a linking theory, which links the ". . . verb + *that*-complement" structure to the "verb's noun + *that*-complement" structure. The linking theory works in many cases; but there are cases, in which the linking theory does not work:

(6) a. John objects that men and women are equal.
b. John's objection that men and women are equal (is supported by many people.)
c. The objection that men and women are equal (. . .).

(7) a. *John facts that the boss was ousted.
b. *John's fact that the boss was ousted (. . .).
c. The fact that the boss was ousted (was shocking to other bosses).

In the case of the head noun *objection*, it can be derived from its cognate verb *object*. However, as seen in (7), such a linking fails in the case of the head noun *fact,* simply because the head noun *fact* lacks its cognate verb. Such head nouns include the following:

(8) doctrine, evidence, fact, idea, issue, notion, policy, problem, property, tenet, thesis, etc.

This syntactic problem cannot be solved by the notion of derivation. Hence, we must regard the construction of "head noun + content clause" as an independent construction.

The head noun and its content clause can be linked by the copula, as mentioned above:

(9) a. the claim that the boss is planning to cut salaries.
b. The claim is that the boss is planning to cut salaries.

(10) a. the idea that semantics based on understanding is superior to semantics based on truth conditions.
b. The idea is that semantics based on understanding is superior to semantics based on truth conditions.

(11) a. the fact that computers are blind to contexts.
b. The fact is that computers are blind to contexts.

This linking of the head noun and the content clause by the copula means that the content clause specifies the head noun.

It should be noted that head nouns are restricted to abstract nouns: concrete nouns cannot be specified by the content clause, although they can be modified by the relative clause. It should also be noted that the same sentence can occur with different head nouns, and conversely, the same head noun can occur with different sentences. This means that the combination of a head noun and a content clause is determined by the speaker's intention. For details, see Yang (1993d).

What was not dealt with in Yang (1993d) is the head noun *question*:

(12) a. John raised the question whether the earth would collide with another star.
b. The question whether the earth will collide with another star arises.
c. The question is whether the earth will collide with another star.
d. The question arises whether the earth will collide with another star.

In (12a, b), *the question* is the head noun, and *whether the earth would/will collide with another star* is the content clause. This claim is supported by sentences (12c) and (12d). In (12c), the head noun and the content clause are linked by copula, like those cited above. Sentence (12d) is derived from sentence (12b) by Extraposition-from-NP, like other cases (cf. Unit 14).

Exercises and problems

1. How do we distinguish between the content clause and the relative clause?
2. Describe the function of the content clause and the relative clause.
3. What is the difference of affirmative head nouns and negative head nouns?
4. Does a pseudo-negative head noun behave like an affirmative head noun or a negative head noun? Why?
5. Why is it that some abstract nouns can serve as head nouns of content clauses, while concrete nouns cannot?
6. Dixon (1991:158) mentions that the *to it* in (a) may be deleted:

    a. I object <u>to it</u> that John wants to play cricket.

    b. I object that John wants to play cricket.

    Q 1: Where does *it* come from? Why is *it* necessary in (a)?

    Q 2: Is there any meaning difference between (a) and (b)? If yes, explain the difference.

    Q 3: If the meaning difference is significant, is *to it* deletable?
7. Do the strings of "head noun + content clause" and "head noun + relative clause" syntactically behave differently or similarly? Describe your answer in detail.

8. Rearrange the words in the parentheses, so that it makes sense in the context:

   Our teacher always tells us that once we begin a work, it should be completed. In this regard, the sentence (never, right, done, things, halves, are, by, done) is very appealing.

9. Is the omissibility of the complementizer *that* in the following sentence generalizable?

   The fact is (that) computers are blind to contexts.

10. Identify head nouns of the following sentence:

    There is no question/objection that rich people are not necessarily generous.

11. Analyze the following sentence:

    It might be objected that rich people are generous.

Unit 12

Heavy Constituent Shift

This rule is also known as Complex Constituent Shift. Since NP is the typical constituent in this rule, the rule is also known as Heavy/Complex NP Shift. The notion of "shift" here means the exchange of positions. In the case of this rule, a heavy constituent and the following light constituent exchange their positions. This shift is functionally motivated. If the shift does not take place, the parsing/understanding of the sentence is difficult. In order to ease the difficulty, the shift takes place.

The following illustrate the rule:

(1) a. He made his position clear.
b. *He made clear his position.

(2) a. *He made that he was interested in the peaceful use of atomic energy clear.
b. He made clear that he was interested in the peaceful use of atomic energy. (Heavy NP Shift)
c. He made it clear that he was interested in the peaceful use of atomic energy. (Extraposition)

In ordinary cases, the object precedes the object complement. Sentence (1b) violates this requirement. In (2a, b), in contrast, the opposite works. Although sentence (2a) meets the requirement, the understanding is difficult because the heavy object separates the object complement too far from the verb. In the case like this, the heavy object and the object complement must exchange their positions, so that the verb and the object complement become closer, which results in sentence (2b). In a situation like this, it is said that sentence (2a) is "grammatical", but not "acceptable". In terms of acceptability, sentence (2c) is better than sentence (2b). Sentence (2c) is derived from (2a) by Extraposition (= Extra), which will be dealt with in Unit 14.

For generalization, I will posit the following principle:

(3) Linkability Principle (LP):
An element may be moved or deleted to the extent that it will be linkable.

For the exposition of this principle, consider the sentences in (2). Sentence (2a) is not acceptable, because the main verb and the object complement are not linkable, owing to the heavy object between them. Sentence (2b) is acceptable because the main verb, the object complement, and the object are linkable. Sentence (2c) is better than (2b) because the main verb, the object *it*, and the object complement are more easily linkable.

Below is another example:

(4) a. *I can only accept that, from birth, a child's mind equips itself more and more adequately by its own working, trial and error, and deliberate experimentation as true.
b. I can only accept as true that . . . (Heavy NP Shift)
c. I can only accept it as true that . . . (Extra)

In (4a), the sentential complement object is so heavy that it is extremely hard to link the main verb and the adjunct *as true*. Hence, it is not acceptable. In order to avoid such a difficulty, Heavy NP Shift must apply, yielding (4b). Here again, the extraposed version (4c) is better than the heavy-NP-shifted version (4b) because the linking is easier.

Heavy NP Shift cannot apply to the subject. Whatever theories argue about this restriction, the reason is very simple. The application of the rule results in the subjectless sentence, which is not allowed. Since Extra leaves its trace, the alternative is to apply Extra to the subject, so that the subjectlessness can be avoided.

Consider the following examples from Dixon (1991:111):

(5) a. She baked a chocolate cake with/using flour, sugar, cocoa, milk, eggs, butter and vanilla.
b. ?She baked the flour, sugar, cocoa, milk, eggs, butter and vanilla essence into a chocolate cake.

Dixon's explanation for the marginality of (5b) is this: it would be implausible to focus on a complex list of cake ingredients. Furthermore, the marginality seems to be also due to the heaviness of the object.

Sells (1985:61) mentions that Chomsky notes (that Postal observed) that Heavy NP Shift applies with *believe*, but not with *want*, which would follow from the fact that "the NP was shifted out of a non-maximal S in the one case but a maximal S' in the other":

(6) a. *They'd believe any candidate who would take the trouble to run in every primary <u>to be foolish</u>.
b. They'd believe <u>to be foolish</u> any candidate who would take the trouble to run in every primary.

(7) a. *They'd want any candidate who would take the trouble to run in every primary <u>to win</u>.
b. *They'd want <u>to win</u> any candidate who would take the trouble to run in every primary.

The ungrammaticality of the (a) sentences is due to the fact that the objects are so heavy that it is hard to link the main verbs to the object complements (*to be foolish*, *to win*). The (b) versions are the results of the application of Heavy NP Shift. As shown above, (6b) is grammatical (where the main verb is *believe*), while (7b) is ungrammatical (where the main verb is want). Whatever theories claim, the reason is very simple:

(8) a. *They'd believe to be foolish/to win the election.
  b. They'd want to be foolish/to win the election.

The verb *believe* cannot be linked with the following infinitive, as shown in (8a). Hence, in (6b), the verb *believe* is linked with the object followed by its complement. This is the reason why (6b) is grammatical for the sense of (6a). In contrast, the verb *want* can be linked with the following infinitive, as shown in (8b). Hence, the original meaning is changed. This is the reason why (8b) is not grammatical. This explanation is not restricted only to the contrast of *believe* and *want*; this explanation can apply to all verbs which behave like *believe* vs. *want* with regard to the following infinitival complement.

The notion of "heaviness" is not easy to define. Sometimes it means the length of the constituent/string; some other times it means complexity of the structure; still some other times it means both.

Consider the following:

(9) a. John invited you'll never guess how many people to his party. (source: McCawley 1988:739)
  b. John invited you'll-never-guess-how-many-people to his party. (hyphenated: mine)

Comparing these two sentences, I guess that (9b) is better than (9a) in terms of acceptability since (9b) is less heavy. In general, if the words of a sentence are linked by hyphens, the whole string functions like a word.

While reading books and articles, I noticed the following examples, in which Heavy NP Shift has applied:

(10) a. We leave open the possibility that an investigation conducted at a more detailed empirical level might find this to be true with *lie*.

b. By taking into account not only the meaning of U, but also the precise mechanisms which may cause a divergence between the meaning of U and what is communicated by the utterance of U in a particular context.

c. Their accounts of meaning share with atomism the position that meaning can be given of lexical items singly, without reference to some larger whole.

d. This would leave unexplained the distributional contrasts that first led Emonds to reject the NP status of *that* clauses.

e. She takes as her primary data a wide variety of uses of negation, many derived from Grice, which are not reducible to garden-variety descriptive negation.

f. Ducrot (1972:175-8) adds to the familiar cases of (57) another variety of metalinguistic conditional statement, exemplified in sentences which translate as follows: . . .

If the object NPs are not heavy in these sentences, the English writers/speakers will never place the underlined parts at the present positions.

Consider the following examples:

(11) a. *We account for the exclusion of 'property modifying' adjectives like *alleged, former, poor, sorry* which do not denote properties at all from postnominal position.

b. We account for the exclusion from postnominal position of 'property modifying' adjectives like *alleged, former, poor, sorry* which do not denote properties at all. [source: JL 30:222]

While reading an article, I noticed sentence (11b). If the NP is not heavy, the grammaticalness of (11a) and (11b) will be reversed, as shown in the following versions:

(12) a. We account for the exclusion of such adjectives <u>from postnominal position.</u>
b. *We account for the exclusion <u>from postnominal position</u> of such adjectives.

Example (11b) is different from others. Heavy NP Shift has been known to apply to sentences/clauses. Nevertheless, Heavy NP Shift also applies within a nominal, as shown in (11b). Thus, the NP shift in example (11b) can be called "Heavy NP Shift in Nominal". But this distinction does not mean that Heavy NP Shift and Heavy NP Shift in Nominal are different kinds.

Exercises and problems

1. Specify the notion of "heaviness".
2. What is the motivation for Heavy Constituent Shift?
3. What is the relation between "linkability" and "heaviness"?
4. Can Heavy NP Shift apply to the subject? If not, why?
5. Is there any relation between Heavy NP Shift and the End-weight maxim?
6. Can Heavy NP Shift apply to the following sentence?
   If not, why? How can we make this sentence acceptable?
   *I expect the students who have well prepared for the exam by reading relevant books and articles to pass.

Unit 13

Particle Movement and Preposition Stranding

Particle Movement

Particle Movement is also known as Particle Separation. The term *particle* here means verbal particle, which is different from preposition. Particles may jump over their objects, by being separated from their verbs, under certain conditions. The following illustrate the rule:

(1) a. In the evening, she usually stood up her date.
    b. In the evening, she usually stood her date up.

(2) a. The accidental shock touched off the explosion.
    b. The accidental shock touched the explosion off.

(3) a. He called up almost all friends from Paris.
    b. He called almost all friends from Paris up.

The rule links the (a) sentences to the (b) sentences, as shown above.

What happens, if the object is heavy? Of course, the rule cannot apply, which is functionally motivated. This restriction goes with the function of Heavy NP Shift, which was dealt with in Unit 12.

(4) a. He called up the man his father met.
    b. ?He called the man his father met up

(5) a. He shot down a man from a village on a mountain in a country.
b. *He shot a man from a village on a mountain in a country down.

(6) a. The strong wind blew over the table which was set up in the garden in order to put food on for birds.
b. **The strong wind blew the table which was set up in the garden in order to put food on for birds over.

The (b) versions clearly show that if the object is heavy, the rule cannot apply, and that the heavier, the worse. The degree of acceptability here is an reflection of the linkability principle (cf. Unit 12).

The unique function of the verbal particle is to help its own verb, to the effect that the verb extends its meaning by taking some particles. This fact strongly suggests that the verbal particle should not be separated from its verb. Then, a serious question is: why do English speakers want to separate the particle from its verb? The unique motivation for the separation seems to get over the pronominal object which is light:

(7) a. *The strong wind blew over it.
b. The strong wind blew it over.

This restriction is motivated by the end-weight maxim, which means that heavy information tends to be placed toward the end of a sentence (cf. Leech 1983:62–66). In other words, light information such as pronouns tends not to be placed toward the end of a sentence.

The end-weight maxim, however, has serious problems. Bolinger (1971) provides a number of examples in which a particle precedes the pronoun, and conjoined pronouns may follow the particle:

(8) a. Fancy takes on him.
b. I bade them to take away you.

c. Bring along him and her.

Sentence (8c) accords with the end-weight maxim, but sentences (8a, b) don't. Wood (1955) also indicates that personal or reflexive pronouns have mid-position, but demonstrative and possessive pronouns take end-position more freely:

(9) a. Whoever else gives up his seat, I shall not give up mine.
b. I want you to take down this.

Van Dongen (1919) indicates that conjoined particles occur finally:

(10) a. He let them (=the dogs) in and out.
b. He recited it (=the poem) over and over.

Considering these examples, we can say that conjoined particles have heavier weight than pronouns. (For general properties of the verb-particle combination, see Fraser (1974).)

Preposition Stranding

Concerning the separation of coherent elements, preposition stranding deserves some description. Prepositions are to "parasite" on nominals (noun, pronoun, gerund). For instance, if a nominal disappears, the preposition usually (but not always) disappears, too:

(11) a. John is very much interested in philosophy as well as linguistics.
b. *John is very much interested in philosophy as well as.
c. John is very much interested in philosophy as well.

Despite this nature, prepositions may be separated from their nouns. This phenomenon is called "preposition stranding", in contrast to "preposition pied-piping".

The following illustrate preposition stranding:

(12) a. The baby-sitter looks after the baby.
     b. The baby is looked after (by the baby-sitter).

(13) a. John went to Waikiki with Susan.
     b. Who(m) did John go to Waikiki with?
     c. With whom did John go to Waikiki?

(14) a. Somebody famous has slept in this bed.
     b. This bed has been slept in by somebody famous.

(15) a. Kim visited UN for some reason.
     b. What did Kim visit UN for? (--> What for?)
     c. For what did Kim visit UN? (--> For what?)

The (c) versions are examples of preposition pied-piping, and the (b) versions are examples of preposition stranding.

Preposition stranding must obey certain constraints. For instance, time and manner prepositions are not allowed to strand, if they don't have a strong link with the verb:

(16) a. At what time did John get up?
     b. *What time did John get up at?

(17) a. In what manner did John scold his son?
     b. *What manner did John scold his son in?

Both in Particle Movement and in Preposition Stranding, the particle and the preposition cannot be separated from the verb and the noun, respectively, if a heavy constituent intervenes between them. This impossibility is due to the linkability. If the space between the separated elements is too distant, the separated elements cannot be linked, which results in the difficulty of understanding.

There are two types of causes for Preposition Stranding. One type is due to the movement of the host nominal; the other is due to the deletion of the host nominal. The examples cited above are of the first type. The second type is illustrated below:

(18) a. (It is) 10 minutes after the hour.
b. (It is) 10 minutes <u>after</u>.

(19) a. The sale price is 10% off the list price.
b. The sale price is 10% <u>off</u>.

The deletion of the host nominal is allowed under the condition that the deleted nominal is predictable.

Thus far, the examples are restricted to Preposition Stranding which is optional. The following, in contrast, illustrate obligatory cases:

(20) a. to sit <u>on</u> the chair.
b. This is the chair for you to sit <u>on</u>.
c. *This is <u>on</u> the chair for you to sit.

(21) a. to cut the cake <u>with</u> a knife.
b. Give me a knife to cut the cake <u>with</u>.
c. *Give me <u>with</u> a knife to cut the cake.

(22) a. to talk <u>to</u> the man.
b. The president is the man for me to talk <u>to</u>.
c. *The president is <u>to</u> the man for me to talk.

The (a) versions show that the underlined prepositions are required in the contexts. Since the (c) versions are impossible, the only alternatives are the (b) versions in which the underlined prepositions are forced to be stranded.

* * *

English prepositions are hard for foreigners to select correctly. Interestingly enough, there are what I call "non-accidental errors" in selecting correct prepositions. There are cases in which non-native speakers of English tend to select redundant prepositions:

(23) a. They approached the terminal.
b. *They approached to the terminal.

(24) a. They attacked the enemy.
b. *They attacked against the enemy.

(25) a. He could answer the question.
b. *He could answer to the question.

(26) a. John married Susan.
b. *John married with/to Susan.

(27) a. John wanted to challenge the tough course.
b. *John wanted to challenge to the tough course.

It is highly probable that non-native speakers tend to choose the ungrammatical (b) versions. Errors of this type are not accidental. When these verbs become their cognate nouns, these nouns can be linked to the object nouns via the same prepositions, as shown below:

(23) c. their approach to the terminal.
(24) c. their attack against the enemy.

(25) c. his answer to the question.
(26) c. John's marriage with/to Susan.
(27) c. John's challenge to the tough course.

In the (c) versions, the underlined prepositions function as linkers. This fact suggests that the linking prepositions are cognitively required. Such cognitive requirement is naturally extended to the linking of "verb + obj noun". Then, the next natural question is whether the redundant insertion of prepositions is universal or learner's language-specific. The answer calls for research.

Examples of the (b) versions of (23–27) must be distinguished from the following:

(28) a. John visited/met his former professor.
b. John visited/met with his former professor.

Here, the preposition *with* is not a redundant insertion. Both (28a) and (28b) are grammatical, and have different meanings.

Exercises and problems

1. Provide examples in which the heavy NP prevents Particle Movement and Preposition Stranding.
2. What is the commonality between Particle Movement and Preposition Stranding?
3. How does the linkability principle work in connection with Particle Movement and Preposition Stranding?
4. Provide examples in which verbs and particles are tightly linked.

5. Provide examples in which verbs and particles are less tightly linked.
6. What is the difference of the following?
    a. Verbs as well as nouns involve frame-semantic meanings.
    b. Verbs, as well as nouns, involve frame-semantic meanings.
7. Why is it that non-native speakers tend to insert redundant prepositions between verbs and objects? Is it universal or learner's language-specific?
8. Check grammaticality/acceptability of the following:
    a. I danced with Susan to Arirang.
    b. With whom did you dance to Arirang?
    c. Whom did you dance with to Arirang?
    d. To what did you dance with Susan?
    e. What did you dance with Susan to?
    f. With whom and to what did you dance?
    g. Whom and what did you dance with and to?

Unit 14

Extraposition and Extraposition-from-NP

Extraposition

The subject or object may move to the end of a sentence, leaving its trace *it*. Such subjects and objects are restricted to sentential and infinitival complements (out of three types of complements), unlike Right-dislocation where NP may move to the end of a sentence. The following illustrate Extra:

(1) a. That the diplomat is not reliable bothers me very much.
    b. It bothers me very much that the diplomat is not reliable.

(2) a. To watch TV for more than one hour a day may be a waste of life.
    b. It may be a waste of life to watch TV for more than one hour a day.
    c. For the odor to wear away takes at least one month.
    d. It takes at least one month for the odor to wear away.

The sentential complement subject is extraposed in (1), and the infinitival complement subjects are extraposed in (2).

Gerundival complement subjects behave differently:

(3) a. John's driving fast is irritating everybody in the back seat.

b. *It is irritating everybody in the back seat John's driving fast. (Extra)
c. It is irritating everybody in the back seat, John's driving fast. (Right-dislocation)

The only difference between (3b) and (3c) is the absence or the presence of a comma. (3b) involves Extraposition, and (3c) involves Right-dislocation. A serious point to note here is that the sentential complement subject and the infinitival complement subject may be extraposed, whereas the gerundival complement subject cannot be extraposed. Concerning the contrast of infinitival complements and gerundival complements, it is generally known that infinitival complements express verb-like actions, while gerundival complements express noun-like events (cf. Yule 1998:217–219). On this basis, we can say that Extra is allowed in the case of actions, but is not allowed in the case of events. This explanation, however, cannot cover sentential complements, since sentential complements seem to express noun-like events rather than verb-like actions.

Furthermore, we can notice some examples, which involve gerundival complements:

(4) Rosenbaum (1967:124)
a. It is useless trying to do that.
b. It is more fun talking to her than kissing her.

(5) Emonds (1972:60)
a. It is fun talking to foreigners.

(6) Postal (1974:14)
a. It is fun calling Sally.
b. It is hard working for RCA.
c. It is useless talking to her.

The reason why these examples are possible is not known. As already indicated above, what is known is that sentential complements and infinitival complements in the subject position are extraposable, while gerundival complements are not. In this regard, examples (4–6) are interesting. My wild speculation is that Extraposition is beginning to extend its application even to gerundival complements. On a second thought, it is a hasty expectation.

Concerning three types of complements, infinitival complements express verb-like actions, gerundival complements express noun-like events, and sentential complements seem to express noun-like events. Especially on the sentential complements, my intuitive judgement might be wrong. According to Ross (1973a:141), sentential complements are closer to infinitival complements rather than to gerundival complements:

(7) Ross's nouniness squish
  a. sentential complement
  b. infinitival complement
  c. gerundial complement
  d. derived nomnal
  e. noun

In (7), we can divide them into two classes: (i) sentential complement and infinitival complement and (ii) gerundial complement, derived nominal, and noun. Then, we can say that the first class allows Extra, while the second class does not. If Ross's "nouniness squish" (7) is correct, the fact that sentential and infinitival complements allow Extra, while gerundival complements and nouns prohibit Extra, is neatly accounted for.

Here, what is not convincing to me is that sentential complements are closer to infinitival complements rather than to gerundival complements.

However, Ross's nouniness squish is established through many rules including Extra. Here, intuition and linguistic fact seem to conflict with each other. On a second thought, however, sentential complements are closer to infinitival complements since sentential and infinitival complements are closer in terms of predication: gerundival complements are less predicative than sentential and infinitival complements. Hence, Ross's nouniness squish is not groundless.

Next, consider the following:

(8) a. I wouldn't guarantee that this medicine will work well.
b. I wouldn't guarantee it that this medicine will work well.

(9) a. *I take that you plan to become a monk.
b. I take it that you plan to become a monk.

(10) a. Politicians know that voters prefer results.
b. *Politicians know it that voters prefer results.

These examples show that, in the case of the object position, Extraposition may optionally apply, as in (8); it must apply, as in (9); or it is not allowed, as in (10). This difference comes from the nature of the main verbs. One class of verbs optionally allows Extra, another class requires Extra, and still another class does not allow Extra. The first class includes: *believe, doubt, expect, resent,* etc. The full list of verbs for three categories call for research. I can just say that Extra in the object position is quite restrictive.

Consider the following:

(11) a. *I <u>take</u> that everybody wants to live a happy life <u>for granted</u>.
b. I <u>take it for granted</u> that everybody wants to live a happy life.

(12) a. *I can only accept that, from birth, a child's mind equips itself more and more adequately by its own working, trial and error, and deliberate experimentation as true.
b. I can only accept it as true that, from birth, a child's mind equips itself more and more adequately by its own working, trial and error, and deliberate experimentation.

(11a) is not acceptable, although grammatical, because the main verb *take* and the adjunct *for granted* are too distant to be linked. In a case like this, the sentential complement is forced to move from the object position toward the end of the sentence. (11b) is acceptable because the main verb and the adjunct are easily linkable. The same thing can be said of example (12). These examples show that Extra is well motivated even in the case of the object position, if the object is so heavy that the verb and the adjunct cannot be linked. Otherwise, the motivation cannot be maintained. Then, what is the source of *it*?

Consider the following:

(13) a. I object that men are stronger than women.
b. *I object to that men are stronger than women.
c. I object to it that men are stronger than women.

(14) a. I see that John is doing his job well.
b. *I see to that John is doing his job well.
c. I see to it that John is doing his job well.

Comparing (13a) and (13c), the content of the sentential complement is not negated in (13a), whereas it is negated in (13c) (cf. Unit 11). This difference is the reflection of the contrast of *object* and *object to*, in connection with the sentential complement. Then, what is the source of *it* in (13c)? One possible source is Extra. The other source is the forced insertion: because a preposition cannot occur with a sentential complement, *it* is forced to be inserted. Thus, two views (the Extra view and the forced insertion view) may be available. Here, the Extra view will respond: that's why Extra is obligatory for *object to*, and the like. The same argumentation is applicable to example (14). Then, the forced insertion view's repartee will be: why does Extra apply only to specific lexical items in the case of object position? This issue calls for further research.

It should be noted that indirect questions may also be extraposed:

(15) a. What John claims is not clear.
b. It is not clear what John claims.

(16) a. I don't know what John claims.
b. *I don't know it what John claims.

(17) a. Who will be elected president is not predictable.
b. It is not predictable who will be elected president.

(18) a. We cannot predict who will be elected president.
b. *We cannot predict it who will be elected president.

As shown above, indirect questions in the subject position can be extraposed, while indirect questions in the object position cannot.

Concerning the source of *it*, my speculation is as follows. Deictically, *this*, *it*, and *that* are used for physical reference, and only *it* is used for mental reference (cf. Yang 1972:246). Since the pronominal trace *it* is used only for mental reference, the source of *it* is the mental use of *it*. I claim that this is also the source of any so-called preparatory *it*.

Finally, I would like to add that Dixon (1991) is a good reference for the relation of verbs and their complements. Grimshaw (1979) is also a relevant reference.

Exercises and problems

1. Sentential and infinitival complements are freely extraposable from the subject position, but they are not so free from the object position in the case of "adjacent Extra". Why?
2. Verbs *object* and *object to* are different with respect to their sentential complements. Describe it in detail.
3. Why is it that gerundival complements in general are not extraposable from the subject position?
4. Compare Heavy NP Shift and Extraposition in structure and function.
5. What rule is involved in the following sentence?

   Why is it that Extraposition and Extraposition-from-NP are similar, if not identical, rules?
6. Explain the following data:

   A: How is it in your room?

   B: a. It is hard to study.

   b. *To study is hard.

Extraposition-from-NP

The notion of head noun is relevant to content clauses and relative clauses. Both structures have the form: "head noun + connector + clause". The string of "connector + clause" may be separated from the head noun, and move toward the end of the sentence. This rule is Extraposition-from-NP. NP here refers either to the head noun of a content clause or to the head noun of a relative clause (cf. Unit 11). Extra and Extra-from-NP are the same, except whether the extraposed material is separated from the head noun or not.

The following illustrate content clause Extra:

(19) a. The thought that I should have studied cybernetics occurred to me.
b. The thought occurred to me that I should have studied cybernetics.

(20) a. A rumor that the superman can destroy all the dangerous weapons has pleased all peace-loving people.
b. A rumor has pleased all peace-loving people that the superman can destroy all the dangerous weapons.

(21) a. The question whether the earth will collide with another star arises.
b. The question arises whether the earth will collide with another star.

(22) a. Permission for the girl student to leave early was granted.
b. Permission was granted for the girl student to leave early.

The underlined clauses are separated from the head nouns of the content clauses. Note that (22) is different from (19–21) in that (22) has an infinitival complement for its content clause. Ordinarily, the content clause takes the sentential complement. But the content clause does not exclude the infinitival complement.

The following illustrate relative clause Extra:

(23) a. The politician who won this year's election is rumored to lose the next election.
b. The politician is rumored to lose the next election who won this year's election.

(24) a. The boss whom the staff respect much is very generous.
b. The boss is very generous whom the staff respect much.

(25) a. An old lady let the cats which were meowing out.
b. An old lady let the cats out which were meowing.

The underlined clauses are separated from the head nouns of the relative clauses. Thus, there is no difference between content clauses and relative clauses, in conjunction with Extra-from-NP.

Jacobs (1975) indicates that if the content clause does not carry new information, Extra-from-NP is blocked:

(26) a. The fact that the city has fallen became known.
b. *The fact became known that the city has fallen.

(27) a. The fact that she lied to the grand jury remains.
b. The fact remains that she lied to the grand jury.

The judgment on the (b) versions stands on the assumption that the content clause of (26b) carries old information, and the content clause of (27b) carries new information. This difference remains to be explained. My wild speculation is that, in the case of "old information", the head noun carries the whole necessary information. Then, the information of the extraposed content clause is redundant.

Hankamer (1973:53) mentions that Ross (1967=1986) contends that Extra-from-NP must be blocked if the extraposed constituent would pass over another NP in being shifted:

(28) a. I gave a kid who was standing there looking hungry a banana.
b. *I gave a kid a banana who was standing there looking hungry.

This constraint seems to be motivated by the worry that the relative clause tends to modify the immediately preceding noun, so that the original meaning changes. Incidentally, sentence (28a) is less acceptable because indirect object and direct object are separated too far. The best version is (28c) below:

(28) c. I gave a banana to a kid who was standing there looking hungry.

It is said that non-restrictive (= appositive) relative clauses cannot be extraposed from head nouns:

(29) a. John, who had been sick for a long time, came in.
b. *John came in, who had been sick for a long time.

The reason, however, is not known. My best guess is that, if Extra-from-NP is allowed for non-restrictive relative clauses, the distinction between "restrictive" and "non-restrictive" relative clauses may become blurred.

Exercises and problems

1. Explain data (29) functionally.
2. What rule is involved in the following sentence? And Why?

   What these approaches have in common is the assumption, pervasive in the literature, that the direct object of a VP is necessarily licensed by the verb.
3. Why is it that content clauses and relative clauses behave similarly, with respect to Extra-from-NP?

Unit 15

Nominal Extraposition

As seen in Unit 14, complements can be extraposed. Similarly, nominals in specific cases look extraposed. Hence, the rule is called Nominal Extraposition (henceforth, NE). McCawley (1988:718–719) indicates that there is a type of exclamative sentence that has the form of an NP with either a relative clause or an *of*-expression, and it can be paraphrased by WH-exclamative:

(1) a. It's amazing the amount of money he spent.
    b. It's amazing what amount of money he spent.

McCawley takes such expressions to be derived from underlying exclamative sentences by "Telescoping", which converts the focus of a WH-exclamative into a corresponding definite NP and the remainder into a restrictive relative clause, e.g. from (1b) to (1a). The term, Nominal Extraposition, might suggest that sentence (1a) is derived from sentence (2a), paralleling with Extraposition:

(2) a. The amount of money he spent is amazing.
    b. It is amazing the amount of money he spent. (=1a)

Here, the nominal *the amount of money he spent* is extraposed to the end of the sentence, leaving behind its trace *it*. The trace is uniformly *it*, regardless of the number of the nominal. Thus, the trace is uniform in all types of Extraposition (except for Extraposition-from-NP). The derivation just described, however, does not hold, simply because there is no paraphrase relation between (2a) and (2b). This matter will be explicated later towards the end of this unit.

For more details, consider the following examples from Michaelis and Lambrecht (1996:215-216, henceforth, M-L):

(3) a. It's amazing the people you see here!
  b. A : Where's Buttsy?
   B : He's slipped in to see Senator what's-his-face.
   A : It's amazing the access he's got!
  c. It's astonishing the age at which they became skilled liars.
  d. It's staggering the number of books that can file up.
  e. It's unbelievable the people who are verbally abusive to fat people.

The examples in (3) contain (i) a focused main verb (= underlined adjectives which receive prosodic peaks) and (ii) a pronominal subject *it*, which "apparently" corefers with a postverbal definite NP.

To put the conclusion first, M-L contend that the sentences in (3) instantiate an "exclamation sentence type" that must be distinguished from Right-dislocation (= RD) on syntactic, semantic and pragmatic grounds.

Syntactically, NE and RD are distinct. The NE construction, unlike RD, does not involve coreference between the pronominal subject *it* and the extraposed NP (cf. 3a, 3e). By contrast, the RD construction requires coreference:

(4) a. They are red leather, the shoes she's wearing. (RD)
  b. *It is red leather, the shoes she's wearing. (RD)

(4b) is not grammatical because it does not meet the requirement of coreference. The pronominal trace *it* does not match with the right-dislocated *shoes*. In contrast, the pronominal subject in NE sentences must always be *it*:

(5) a. It's amazing the things you see here! (NE)
b. *They're amazing the things you see here! (NE)

(5b) is not grammatical because the pronominal subject is not *it*.

In the case of RD, an instance missing the dislocated constituent is always a syntactically well formed and potentially complete sentence. In NE, in contrast, this is not the case, although this is not always obvious from an exclusively structural point of view. Features of prosody support the view that the postpredicate NP in NE is indispensable. This NP is necessarily accented. In RD, the postpredicate NP has a low and flat intonation contour, indicating that it follows the right boundary of the VP focus domain.

Another argument in favor of distinguishing NE from RD concerns the type of determiners. Fillmore and Kay (1993, Chapter 10) observe the following contrast:

(6) a. It's <u>amazing</u> the things children say. (NE)
b. It's <u>amazing</u> what things children say.

(7) a. They're <u>amazing</u>, the things children say. (RD)
b. *They're <u>amazing</u>, what things children say.

As (6b) shows, the determiner *what* may occur in exclamative sentences that closely resemble NE, the NP *what things children say* being semantically equivalent to the NP *the things children say* in (6a). In RD, by contrast, this determiner may not occur (cf. 7b). The equivalence between (6a) and (6b) stems from the fact that NE is closely related formally and semantically to an extraposition construction that has an exclamative function and licenses a clausal complement having the form of an indirect question.

For other distinctions between NE and RD, see M-L (1996:223–225).

Now semantic aspects of NE are in order. M-L contend that the NE construction has an exclamative function, and its scalar properties follow from this function. They define exclamative utterances as: "those in which the speaker (i) presupposes that some entity is located at some point on a property scale, and (ii) asserts that the entity manifests a remarkable high degree of this property". The affective stance involved is generally expressed by a subordinate main predicator. These predicators evoke expectation contravention; they contain AP complements like *amazing*, *astonishing*, *incredible*, *unbelievable*, and the like.

The paraphrase set in (8) below shows that NE can be identified with more familiar exclamative constructions:

(8) a. It's amazing the odd people my sister knows.
b. My sister knows so many odd people!
c. It's amazing how many odd people my sister knows.
d. I'm amazed at how many odd people my sister knows.

Each of these sentences asserts that the set of odd people known to my sister ranks high on a numerical scale.

Sentence (8a) is vague in a way that others are not. In (8a), the interpreter must infer the relevant scalar parameter, as well as the corresponding property scale. It is not the odd people themselves but their number that is placed at the extreme end of a number scale. The vagueness inherent in (8a) becomes evident when we note that the relevant scalar parameter could in fact be the variety rather than the number of strange acquaintances. Therefore, (8a) has either of the following paraphrases:

(9) a. It's amazing the variety of odd people.
b. It's amazing the number of odd people.

In the following, subject-predicate sentences are contrasted with their apparent NE counterparts:

(10) a. The odd people my sister knows are amazing.
b. It's amazing the odd people my sister knows.

(11) a. The people who are verbally abusive to fat people are unbelievable.
b. It's unbelievable the people who are verbally abusive to fat people.

(12) a. The age at which they become skilled liars is astonishing.
b. It's astonishing the age at which they become skilled liars.

In the subject-predicate sentence (10a), the property of *being amazing* is predicated of the set of people known to my sister, not of the variety or number of such people, as in the NE sentence (10b). Similar remarks can be made about the difference between (a's) and (b's) of (11) and (12). In the subject-predicate sentence (11a), it is the people who are verbally abusive to obese people that are characterized as being unbelievable, not the high number of such people, as in the NE sentence (11b). The subject-predicate sentence (12a) attributes the property of being astonishing to a particular life stage, or perhaps to the behavior of children at that life stage. The NE sentence (12b), by contrast, is a comment on the early attainment of a life stage; the NP *the age at which they become skilled liars* is interpreted as encoding a particular point on a scale that ranks stages of development according to how early they are manifested.

What the subject-predicate sentences (10a, 11a, 12a) have in common is that they are topic-comment sentences rather than degree exclamations. In the case of complement extraposition, we expect paraphrase relations between subject-predicate sentences and extraposed versions of a given proposition (cf. Unit 14):

(13) a. That John is innocent is obvious. (subject-predicate S)
b. It is obvious that John is innocent. (extraposed S)

In the case of NE, this paraphrase relation does not exist. M-L (1996:244–245) contend that the NE sentence is an instance of the exclamative sentence type. This means that NE sentences are not derived from subject-predicate sentences. In this regard, the term "Nominal Extraposition" is strange and confusing: it just means that NE sentences look like "extra-posed" sentences. The term "Nominal Extraposition", however, does not involve the notion of "derivation". Our curiosity is about the source of *it*, which is the subject of an NE. I regard *it* as a preparatory *it*. Then, its source is the mental use of *it*, as specified in Unit 14. (For pragmatic and discourse aspects of NE constructions, see M-L (1996).)

Exercises and problems

1. What are syntactic distinctions between subject-predicate sentences and NE sentences?
2. What are semantic distinctions between subject-predicate sentences and NE versions?
3. Can a subject-predicate sentence and a NE sentence be paraphrased?
4. On what grounds, do M-L contend that the NE construction is an instance of an exclamation sentence type?
5. What is the source of the subject *it* of NE?
6. Compare RD and NE constructions in detail.

Unit 16

Denominal Verbs

We see that so many lexical items in a dictionary are used for more than one category. For instance, a word can function as a noun, a verb, and an adjective. A serious question is whether the word began to be used as noun, verb, and adjective at the same time, or one of them began to be used first and then it was extended to other categories. Obviously, the latter is the correct answer. Interestingly, this process of lexical extension takes place without the temporal boundary, and will continue forever in the future. This accords with the saying that necessity is the mother of invention. The next question is which category emerges first and then extends to other categories. In most cases, nouns emerge first. There are special cases in which verbs emerge first and then extend to nouns.

The fact that nouns emerge first is not accidental: human beings cognitively recognize things most easily, and then develop relevant actions on them. This process takes two different courses. In one course, people develop lexically or morphologically different forms of verbs from nouns. In the other course, in contrast, people use the same forms of nouns for their cognate verbs. Verbs which are developed from the same forms of nouns are referred to as "denominal verbs", which means that a verb is derived from a cognate noun.

Consider the following:

(1) a. Who can <u>bell</u> the cat?

b. Nobody will <u>stone</u> the conscientious politician.

c. Mother did not blanket her child at a cold night.
d. Mary will winter in Hawaii next year.

Native speakers of English will immediately judge that the underlined words are nouns in zero context. However, they will also immediately recognize the underlined words in (1) as verbs. This means that the underlined words are used as denominal verbs. The VPs in (1a–d) mean *place a bell on the cat's neck*, *throw a stone at the politician*, *cover the child with a blanket*, and *spend a winter in Hawaii*, respectively. What makes such uses and understandings possible? The simple answer is that nouns have such verbal properties.

The above answer is very vague. The more specific answer is that nouns have certain verbal semantic properties. Among them is a salient property, which is transferred to the denominal verb. How can we identify such salient semantic properties of nouns? Nouns have their images, which are perceptualized by native speakers. This is demonstrated in (1). If the salient properties are not shared by native speakers, nouns cannot be freely used as verbs.

The denominal verbalization was systematically studied by Clark and Clark (1979) (henceforth, C-C). Their theory "asserts that there is a convention that speakers and listeners follow in uttering and interpreting such verbs. The convention is that when a speaker utters such a verb, he intends his listener to see that the verb picks out a readily computable and unique kind of state, event, or process that the speaker is confident the listener can figure out–on the basis of the verb itself, the linguistic context, and other mutual knowledge" (C-C 1979:768).

I will now present C-C's categories of denominal verbs. What C-C call "locatum" verbs are ones whose "parent nouns" are in the objective case in clauses that describe the location of one thing with respect to another:

(2) a. Jane blanketed the bed.
    b. Jane did something to cause it to come about that [the bed had one or more blankets on it].

C-C call the clause in square brackets "parent clause", which is the paraphrase of the denominal verb. Some more examples are:

(2) c. turf the yard, cork his face, silver the dish, personnel the office, rime the window, robe the child, yoke the oxen, initial the memo, badge the members, pearl the headdress, etc.

The following illustrates a location verb :

(3) a. John kenneled the dog
    b. John did something to cause it to come about that [the dog was in a kennel].

Here again, the parent clause is locative, but the parent location (*kennel*) corresponds to the surface verb, and the parent locatum (*dog*) to the surface object. This pattern is just the reverse of locatum verbs. Some more examples are:

(3) c. ground the plane, doormat the boots, hook the cups, tender the balloon, book the flight, bulletin the news, blueprint the plans, floor his opponent, island the travellers, etc.

The following illustrates a duration verb:

(4) a. Julia summered in Paris.

b. Julia did something to cause it to come about that [Julia was in Paris for a summer].

Like location verbs, duration verbs have parent nouns in prepositional phrase. The parent noun, however, must denote a stretch of time and take a preposition like *for*. This nature rules out points of time, like *noon* and *midnight*. Qualifications are not compatible with the stretch of time, as shown in (4c):

(4) c. *Julia summered for a week in Paris.

(4c) is not well-formed, because the stretch of summer and that of a week are not compatible. Although most duration verbs are intransitive, some can be transitive too, as shown in (4d):

(4) d. Washington wintered his troops at Valley Forge.

Some more examples are:

(4) e. holiday in France, weekend at the cabin, honeymoon in Hawaii, Christmas in London, New Year in Seoul, Thanks-giving with his parents, jetlag from Sydney to London, etc.

The following illustrates an agent verb:

(5) a. John <u>butchered</u> the cow.
b. John did to the cow the act that one would normally expect [a butcher to do to a cow].

With agent verbs, the parent nouns are in the agentive case. The parent noun is an agent. Some more examples are:

(5) c. jockey the horse, referee the game, umpire the match, chair the meeting, nursemaid the baby, valet the square, police the park, emcee the show, general the army, etc.

The following illustrates a goal verb:

(6) a. Edward powdered the aspirin.
b. Edward did something to cause it to come about that [the aspirin was powder].

In (6b) the powder comes to exist because of Edward's action, and so powder is in the goal case. When the verb is transitive, the parent clause specifies both a source (*aspirin*) and a goal (*powder*). The source denotes the substance from which the goal is made. When the verb is intransitive, the parent clause specifies only a goal. The important characteristic of the goal verbs is their factivity; the shape, entity, form, or role denoted by the parent noun comes to exist by virtue of the action denoted by the verb. Some more examples are:

(6) c. sucker the public, scapegoat the Jews, dupe the voter, outlaw the thief, saint the reformer, god the hero, monk the man, carpool the people, accordion the curtains, etc.

The following illustrates a source verb:

(7) a. Mary pieced the quilt together.
b. Mary did something to cause it to come about that [the quilt is together out of pieces].

The parent clause of (7b) means *put the quilt together from pieces*. Here *piece* denotes the substance from which the quilt is formed, and is therefore in the source case. Some more examples are:

(7) c. word the sentence, letter the sign

The following illustrates an instrument verb:

(8) a. John bicycled into town.
b. John caused it to come about that he was in town by doing the act one would normally expect [one to do with a bicycle].

In (8b), *a bicycle* is in the instrument case; so *bicycled* in (8a) is an instrument verb. Some more examples are:

(8) c. taxi, yacht, canoe, staple, cement, seat-belt, web his clothes to the wall, hasp the door, buckle his belt, thong the sandals on, broom the floor, floss his teeth, soap-and-water his hands, hammer the nail, ruler the child's hand, razor off his beard, toothpick the clam, TNT the building, M-1 the sniper, collar the dog, block the road, track the criminal, etc.

Instrument verbs are distinguished from locatum and location verbs in the way they form antonyms. Marchand (1969:134–5) observes that *de-* and *dis-* can be used with locatum and location verbs. When added to locatum verbs, they result in "privative verbs" like *defrost* and *disarm*; when added to location verbs, they result in "ablative verbs" like *deplane* and *disbar*. In effect, they add a negative to the parent clause of the positive verbs *frost*, *arm*, and *plane* (*bar* cannot stand alone).

In contrast, the negative prefixes *de-* and *dis-* cannot be added to instrument verbs. To make instrument verbs "reversative", *un-* must be added, as in *unglue* and *unshackle* (although *un-* can be added to locatum verbs, as in *unsaddle*). Thus, *debuttoning* a shirt is different from *unbut-*

toning a shirt. In *debuttoning*, one takes buttons off, but in *unbuttoning*, one unfastens buttons. Whether an "*un*-verb" can be a reversative or not is determined by the pragmatic factor (cf. Yang 1998:38–40).

Dictionaries contain denominal verbs. This means that they are lexicalized denominal verbs. Native speakers' linguistic creativity, however, always gets over the lexical items in the dictionary. For example,

(9) a. Don't Hitler my territory.
 b. He is Monday-morning-quarterbacking on the matter.

When confronted with these sentences, (near-)native speakers of English can easily interpret them, although any dictionary does not contain *Hitler* and *Monday-morning-quarterback* as verbs. Even the following sentence can also be interpreted by rather sensitive speakers (cf. Yang 1998:17–18):

(9) c. He is Friday-evening-quarterbacking on the matter.

This possibility suggests that denominal verbs can be divided into two categories:

(10) a. Lexicalized/Idiomatized denominal verbs
 b. Innovative denominal verbs

Of course, the currently lexicalized/idiomatized denominal verbs were originally innovative ones. For instance, some proper nouns were originally used innovatively as verbs, which are now lexicalized:

(11) a. Captain Boycott → boycott
 b. Judge Lynch → lynch
 c. Governor Gerry → gerry + Salamander → gerrymander

The following illustrate innovative denominal verbs from proper nouns (cf. C-C 1979:783):

(12) a. to Shylock $2,700 from the $17,000 raised. = (well-known)
b. The wind Bernoullis around the building. = speeds up according to Bernoulli's Law
c. We then Kleinschmidted the DNA. = used a method of visualizing DNA developed by him
d. A conductor simply Elvira Madigans the movement to death. = conducts soppily, as in the film Elvira Madigan
e. I wanted to Rosemary Woods out that conversation. = erase as Woods is alleged to have done
f. You're in danger of being Hieronymus Bosched. = put in a nightmare setting
g. He is Svengli-ing her to death; She wasn't Krishina'd out. = She was only hippied out (affected as a member of the Krishna sect)
h. the perils of Don Juaning = She seemingly malapropped.
i. We all Wayned and Cagneyed. = to buy breathing space from the guy who really did like to fight
j. I TWAed to New York. = flied to New York by TWA
k. She Ajaxed the sink. = washed the sink using Ajax
l. The canoe Titanicked on a rock in the river. = was sunken

It is not the case that all of those innovative denominal verbs can survive as lexical denominal verbs. For them to survive as lexical denominal verbs requires certain conditions. I posit three conditions. First, the appropriate linguistic context is required. Here the context refers to the sentential elements except the verb slot. The innovative denominal verb functions as the filler for the appropriate verbal gap. If the appropriate context is lacking, nouns cannot be used as verbs. Second, mutual understanding (= cooperation) between the speaker and the hearer is required. If the hearer cannot understand the speaker's use of innovative denominal verbs, nouns cannot survive as lexicalized denominal verbs. Third, for nouns to be used as verbs requires the verbal gap. If the appropriate verb exists, the innovative denomial verb cannot survive. For instance, the innovative denominal verb *Hitler* in (9a) cannot survive as a lexical denominal verb, because the appropriate verb *invade* exists. In contrast, the denominal verbs in (11) have survived from the innovative denominal verbs, because no appropriate verbs exist. In short, we can use nouns as verbs in appropriate contexts, but whether they can survive as lexical verbs depends on whether they meet the requirements indicated above. In this regard, common nouns are not exceptions. For the distinction of proper nouns and common nouns in terms of some theoretical matters, see C-C (1979).

Exercises and problems

1. What properties are required for nouns to function as verbs?
2. Describe conditions under which initially innovative denominal verbs become obsolete.
3. What happens if the hearer cannot understand the speaker's use of a certain noun as a verb?
4. What is the merit of denominal verbs?
5. Describe the process of denominal verbalization in your mother tongue.
6. Explain the following data in terms of uni-/bi-directionality:
   a. pitted/(*)depitted prune, boned/deboned fish
   b. salted/desalted water, militarized/demilitarized zone, caffeinated/de-caffeinated coffee

7. Explain the difference of the following sentences:

    a. He was not crowned.

    b. He was uncrowned.

8. Can verbs be used as nouns? Is "deverbal nominalization" involved in the following examples?

    a. Mary had a walk in the garden.

    b. Susan had a swim in the river.

    c. John gave the rope a pull.

    d. Susan gave the child a carry.

    e. Bill took a tumble.

    f. Harry took a punch in the stomach.

Unit 17

Dative Shift

Dative constructions have been widely and deeply studied. But this does not mean that there is no room for further study. A dative sentence has double objects: direct object (DO) and indirect object (IO). Dative Shift, which is also known as Dative Movement, exchanges the positions of the two objects. In this process, DOs keep the same form, whereas IOs get prepositions:

(1) a. John gave Mary a humor book.
    b. John gave a humor book to Mary.

(2) a. John bought Mary a humor book.
    b. John bought a humor book for Mary.

The (a) versions are called "double object" dative constructions (or sentences), whereas the (b) versions are called "oblique object" dative constructions (or sentences). In the (b) sentences, IOs have prepositions: *to* in (1) and *for* in (2).

This difference is due to the verbs. Verbs which behave like *give* are "*to*-dative verbs" (simply, *to*-datives), or recipient datives, and verbs which behave like *buy* are "*for*-dative verbs" (simply, *for*-datives), or beneficiary datives:

(3) a. *to*-datives: give, hand, lend, offer, pass, send, show, teach, tell, throw, etc.

b. *for*-datives: buy, build, carve, choose, cook (bake, boil, fry, roast, etc.), fix, get, make, order, save, spare, etc.

For the distinction of the two classes of dative verbs, one way is to "memorize" them item by item. This method is not a bad one. However, there are so many important things and matters to memorize that the memorization method is not the best way. Hence, the better alternative is called for. It is to know the principles. In the case of *to*-datives, DOs are "directly" transferred to IOs by the subject. In the case of *for*-datives, the subject does the transitive verb's action and then gives the product (= DO) to IO. For example, *buy* means (i) buy something, and (ii) give it to somebody. Or *make* means (i) make something, and (ii) give it to somebody. In these examples, we see that two steps are involved: one is the action of the transitive verb itself in the sense of the single object, and the other is the action of "giving". What is in common among *for*-datives is the second step, the action of "giving".

This suggests that *for*-datives allow lexical decomposition:

(4) a. X buys me a book.
    b. X buys a book and gives it to me.
    c. X gives a book to me by buying it.

(5) a. X makes me a kite.
    b. X makes a kite and gives it to me.
    c. X gives a kite to me by making it.

(6) a. X fixes me a sandwich.
    b. X fixes a sandwich and gives it to me.
    c. X givse a sandwich to me by fixing it.

(7) a. X types me a letter.

b. X types a letter and gives it to me.
c. X gives a letter to me by typing it.

It is traditionally known that *to*-datives involve "directness", and *for*-datives involve "indirectness". This traditional distinction is not groundless: the above analysis of two types of datives accords with such a traditional distinction.

The lexical decomposition done above can also apply to rather non-concrete cases:

(8) a. X sings me Arirang.
b. X sings Arirang and gives a certain mental benefit (e.g. being amused) to me.
c. X gives a certain mental benefit to me by singing Arirang.

(9) a. X does me a favor.
b. X does a favor and gives a certain mental benefit (e.g. being helped) to me.
c. X gives a certain mental benefit to me by doing a favor.

It is generally recognized that lexical decomposition is scholars' mental exercise. Nevertheless, the above practice clearly shows us that lexical decomposition has practical use as well. The verbs in (3b) have double functions: (i) transitive verbs, which take single objects (= DOs), and (ii) beneficiary dative verbs, which take two objects (= DOs and IOs). What is shared by the two functions of those verbs is the same DOs. This fact can naturally be captured by invoking lexical decomposition. What are "explicitly" shown up by lexical decomposition of *for*-datives are (i) the difference/similarity between *for*-datives and their cognate transitive verbs and (ii) the difference/similarity between *for*-datives and *to*-datives. For the practical use of lexical decomposition, see Lakoff (1970a) and Yang (1995, 1999b).

It should specially be noted that Goldberg (1992:50, 1995:32–35) claims that many ditransitive expressions do not strictly imply that the second object (= DO) is successfully transferred to the first object (= IO). For example, *Chris baked Jan a cake* does not strictly imply that Jan actually receives the cake. It can only mean that Chris intends to give Jan the cake. Based on this judgment, one might raise the objection that my lexical decomposition is not adequate.

Even if Goldberg's claim is true, my lexical decomposition can hold its ground. We can easily remedy my lexical decomposition by adding one component "Intend" to the component "Giving", like "Intend to Give". This remedy is relevant only to concrete cases (4–7): in non-concrete cases (8, 9), the transfer of DO to IO is guaranteed. One might object that the transfer cannot be successfully executed if the recipient is deaf in (8). My reply is that sentences like (8) are not uttered in such situations. Goldberg (1995:32) indicates that transfer under consideration is rather a *ceteris paribus* implication, but not a strict implication. This statement saves my lexical decomposition, because propositions/sentences without universal quantifiers are normally produced and understood in terms of (i) the limited number or (ii) generic expressions rather than universal expressions.

There are cases in which dativity depends on the VAR (verb and the rest, cf. Unit 10) rather than the verb alone:

(10) a. They <u>gave me</u> a party.
b. *They gave a party <u>to me</u>.
c. They gave a party <u>for me</u>.

It is generally recognized that *give* is the representative (= prototypical) member of *to*-datives, and *buy* is the representative member of *for*-datives.

Nevertheless, this generalization does not hold for (10), because *give* here behaves as a *for*-dative. This is a forced change from *to* to *for* because of *party*, which cannot be transferred. Here my (1999b) lexical decomposition analysis goes as follows:

(11) a. They gave me a party.
b. They held a party and gave a certain mental benefit (e.g. respect, or congratulations) to me.
c. They gave a certain mental benefit to me by holding a party.

In connection with the difference between *to*-datives and *for*-datives, Lakoff and Ross (1976:106) argue that "*to*-NP" belongs inside VP, and "*for*-NP", outside VP. Their "*Do-So* test" goes as follows:

(12) a. John gave a book to Peter, and I did so, too.
b. *John gave a book to Peter, and I did so to Mary.

(13) I bought a car for John, and I'll do so for you, too.

The *do so* of *Do-So* rule refers to VP. In (12a), *do so* refers to "give a book to Peter", which is a VP. In (12b), *do so* also refers to "give a book to Peter". Then, *I did so to Mary* is equivalent to "I gave a book <u>to Peter to Mary</u>", which becomes nonsense. Hence, (12b) is not grammatical. In (13), *I'll do so for you* means "I'll buy a car for you", which does not result in any nonsense. Thus, their argument accords with the traditional distinction of directness and indirectness (cf. Unit 28).

Returning now to the examples in (10), Larson (1988:369) indicates that the oblique and double object alternation (= dative alternation) is not fully productive:

(14) a. John donated the money to charity.

b. *John donated charity the money.

(15) a. The judge spared John the ordeal.
b. *The judge spared the ordeal to John.

This non-alternation depends on individual verbs:

(16) a. contribute, donate (= give away), distribute (= give out), etc.: occur in the oblique dative sentence, but have no double object counterparts.
b. spare, envy, etc.: occur in the double object dative sentence, but have no oblique counterparts.

The following examples are from Green (1974):

(17) a. Mary gave John a cold.
b. *Mary gave a cold to John.

(18) a. Mary gave John a broken arm.
b. *Mary gave a broken arm to John.

(19) a. Mary gave John a black eye.
b. *Mary gave a black eye to John.

(20) a. Mary gave John a bath.
b. *Mary gave a bath to John.

(21) a. Mary gave John a kiss.
b. *Mary gave a kiss to John.

The (b) versions, which are oblique object dative sentences, are not grammatical. This is not due to the verb. As mentioned above in connection with (10), dativity here is sensitive to VAR rather than the verb alone. NPs such as *a cold*, *a broken arm*, *a black eye*, *a bath*, *a kiss*, etc. cannot be transferred from X to Y. This seems to be the reason for the ungrammaticality of the (b) versions. That is, untransferable NPs occur in the double object dative construction, but not in the oblique object dative construction. Thus, the notion of physical "transferability" plays an important role for the distribution of dative constructions.

In connection with the syntactic distinction of the two versions of dative constructions–double object dative constructions vs. oblique object dative constructions, Green (1974) claims that the two versions are also semantically distinct. In the case of double object dative sentences, subjects affect IOs by DOs. But in the case of oblique object dative sentences, such affection is not guaranteed, especially in the case of verbs such as *teach* and *show*:

(22) a. I teach my students Korean traditional wisdom.
b. I teach Korean traditional wisdom to my students.

In (22a), students get wisdom by my teaching. In (22b), in contrast, such a learning is not guaranteed; students may or may not get wisdom by my teaching.

There is some difference in the following:

(23) a. I sent a letter to New York.
b. I sent New York a letter.

In (23a), the primary interpretation of *New York* is the name of a place, and secondarily it may refer to an organization. (23b) is grammatical only if *New York* is interpreted as something like "the New York office of our company". This difference also supports Green's claim.

Now consider the following examples:

(24) a. I gave Bill a book for his mother.
b. I gave a book to Bill for his mother.
c. I gave a book to his mother via Bill.

(25) a. I bought Bill a book for his mother.
b. *I bought a book for Bill for his mother.

(24a, b) mean (24c). Such an indirect transfer is not possible in the form of the oblique object dative sentence (25). The reason seems to be due to the repetition of the adjacent similar form, which causes interpretation to be confusing.

Some speakers do not allow IOs to be extracted, regardless of the extraction construction:

(26) a. You gave somebody perfume.
b. *Who did you give [e] perfume? (Question Formation)

(27) a. the woman. I gave the woman perfume.
b. *the woman who I gave [e] perfume. (Relativization)

(28) a. I dated more women. He gave some women perfume.
b. *I dated more women than he gave [e] perfume. (Comparative)

(29) a. I gave Joan perfume.
b. *Joan, I gave [e] perfume. (Topicalization)

(30) a. I gave Joan perfume.
b. *It was Joan who/that I gave [e] perfume. (Clefting)

It seems to me that this constraint is not groundless. If the IO is extracted from the source structure "Subj - Verb - IO - DO", the source structure is reduced to the structure "Subj - Verb - DO". In the reduced structure, the Verb tends to link to DO, and the DO becomes to function as an ordinary object. As a result, the reduced structure is identical to the ordinary transitive structure. Since the parsing is closed, the extracted IO becomes an orphan, which causes some confusion in terms of interpretation of the whole sentence. If this explanation is not adequate, some alternative adequate explanation is called for. For the difference of IOs of *to*-NP and IOs of *for*-NP with respect to VP constituent, see Unit 28.

Concerning restrictiveness, beneficiary dative (= *for*-dative) constructions are more restrictive than recipient dative (= *to*-dative) constructions. The following data are from Jackendoff and Culicover (1971).

Recipient dative (= *to*-dative) sentences:

(31) a. John gave a book to Mary.
b. What did John give [e] to Mary?
c. Whom did John give a book to [e]?

(32) a. John gave Mary a book.
b. What did John give Mary [e]?
c. *Whom did John give [e] a book?

(33) a. A book was given to Mary by John.
b. What [e] was given to Mary by John?
c. Whom was a book given to [e]?

(34) a. Mary was given a book by John.
b. What was Mary given [e] by John?
c. Who [e] was given a book by John?

(35) a. A book was given Mary by John.
b. What [e] was given Mary by John?
c. *Whom was a book given [e] by John?

Beneficiary dative (= *for*-dative) sentences:

(36) a. John bought a book for Mary.
b. What did John buy [e] for Mary?
c. Whom did John buy a book for [e]?

(37) a. John bought Mary a book.
b. What did John buy Mary [e]?
c. *Whom did John buy [e] a book?

(38) a. A book was bought for Mary by John.
b. What [e] was bought for Mary by John?
c. Whom was a book bought for [e] by John?

(39) a. Mary was bought a book by John.
b. ?What was Mary bought [e] by John?
c. Who [e] was bought a book by John?

(40) a. *A book was bought Mary by John.
b. *What [e] was bought Mary by John?
c. *Whom was a book bought [e] by John?

Exercises and problems

1. Compare the recipient dative sentence and the beneficiary dative sentence.
2. Justify the practical use of lexical decomposition.
3. How do we distinguish between *to*-datives and *for*-datives?
4. Specify the differences of double object dative sentences and oblique object dative sentences.
5. Which constructions are more restrictive between double object dative constructions and oblique object dative constructions? Why?
6. Some speakers do not allow IOs to be extracted. Why?

7. Is the following a case of metalinguistic negation? (cf. Unit 8)

   A: You taught us English syntax and semantics.

   B: I didn't teach you English syntax and semantics.

   I taught English syntax and semantics to you.

8. Why is it that prepositions are required in the process of Dative Shift?
9. What is the major difference between generic expressions and universal expressions?

Unit 18

Quantifier Floating

Quantifier Floating (Q-Floating) is also known as Quantifier Postposing. This rule moves pre-nominal quantifiers to the post-nominal position. Quantifiers include the following:

(1) Quantifiers: *all, every, each, both, many, some, one,* etc.

It is not the case that all quantifiers are involved in Q-Floating. Quantifiers involved in Q-Floating are restricted to the following:

(2) Quantifiers involved in Q-Floating: *all, each, both*

The following illustrate the rule:

(3) a. All (of) my brothers have been practicing taekwondo.
    b. My brothers all have been practicing taekwondo.
    c. My brothers have all been practicing taekwondo.

(4) a. Each of them spent one million dollars on the election.
    b. *Each them spent one million dollars on the election.
    c. They each spent one million dollars on the election.

In (3), the rule links (a) to (b) or (c). In (4), (b) is ill-formed, but (c) is well-formed. This difference suggests that the rule has some constraints.

Let me jump to Maling's (1976:713) summary:

(5)		NP [-pro]	NP [+pro]
a.	Source	all of the men	all of them
		both of the men	both of them
		each of the men	each of them
b.	*of*-Deletion	all the men	*all them
		both the men	*both them
		*each the men	*each them
c.	Q-Pro Flip	(not relevant)	they/them all
			they/them both
			*they/them each
d.	Q-Floating	the men all	they/them all
		the men both	they/them both
		the men each	they/them each

NP[-pro] refers to nouns, and NP[+pro] refers to pronouns. The source forms in (5a) can become the (5b) forms by the optional *OF*-Deletion. Here, *OF*-Deletion applies only to "*all/both* - noun". The ill-formed "Q-pronoun" in (5b) must be changed to the well-formed "pronoun-Q" in (5c) by the obligatory Q-Pro Flip, which exchanges the positions of Q and Pro. The "Q-NP" forms in (5b) can optionally be changed to the "NP-Q" forms in (5d) by the optional Q-Floating.

Notice that the results of Q-Pro Flip in (5c) and of Q-Floating in (5d) look overlapping if the NP is a pronoun, and Q is *all* or *both*. However, that is not overlapping, because Q-Pro Flip (Maling 1976:712) applies to the sequence of "Q-pronoun without the following phrase", where Q refers to *all* or *both*, but not *each*, whereas Q-Floating applies to the sequence of "Q-NP with the following phrase", where NP refers to nouns or pronouns. The term "following phrase" will be clarified below in conjunction with Maling's condition (A).

The above summary accommodates conditions on Q-Floating. Maling (1976:715) posits some conditions on Q-Floating:

Condition (A)

Q-Floating cannot apply to an NP in sentence-final position:

(6) a. Joe was arrested by all/both the cops.
b. *Joe was arrested by the cops all/both.

(7) a. I talked about campus politics with all/both/each of them.
b. *I talked about campus politics with all/both/each them.
c. *I talked about campus politics with them all/both/each.

(8) a. I like all/both/each of the men.
b. I like all/both/*each the men.
c. *I like the men all/both/each.

Sentences (6b), (7c), and (8c) are ungrammatical because Q-Floating has applied at the end of the sentence. In this regard, Sag (1978:147) observes parallelism between lexical contraction (cf. Unit 30) and Q-Floating. Note that lexical contraction here is referred to as structural contraction in Unit 30. Lexical contraction cannot take place immediately before an extraction site; likewise, floated quantifiers cannot immediately precede an extraction site:

(9) a. I don't know what they {all are, *are all} [e].
a'. I don't know what they are all about [e].
b. I know a first grader who has finished more lesson units than the second graders {all have, *have all} [e].
c. None of them were patriots, but chauvinists they {all were, *were all} [e].
d. The more unhappy you say they are, the happier they {all are, *are all} [e].

e. They said our children would be polite and polite they {all are, *are all} [e].

Sag's observation is interesting, but the reasons are not provided. I believe that the restriction is not accidental. The reason that contraction cannot take place before an extraction site is provided in Unit 30. The reason that floated quantifiers cannot immediately precede an extraction site is due to the meaning change: e.g. *they all are* [e] → *they are all* [e].

Maling's condition (A) can accommodate Sag's data (9). Condition (A) requires some constituent to the right of the quantified NP for the Q to float; that target constituent can be any of the major syntactic categories: NP, AP, PP, and VP.

(10) a. Mother gave the kids all some candy to keep them quiet.
b. The guest promised the kids each a quarter.
c. Father bought the twins both bicycles for Christmas.
d. Mother found the boys all so dirty when she got home, that she made them all take a bath.
e. We consider the couple both unbearably pompous.
f. Cinderella's fairy godmother turned the pumpkins all into handsome coaches.
g. He made his money all in platypus platinum.
h. She called the men both bastards.
i. Hang your coats all/both up on hangers.

The examples in (10) satisfy condition (A), and they are grammatical. That is, the underlined quantifiers occur after NPs, which means that Q-Floating has applied to each of them, and some constituent follows the floated quantifier. The ungrammatical examples in (9) violate condition (A). That is, the floated quantifiers are not followed by some constituents. Let us call the phrase after the floated quantifier "the following phrase" (= Maling's "target constituent"). Condition (A) is very interesting, but the explanation has not yet been provided in the literature. My own explanation will be provided at the end of this unit.

Maling (1976:715) indicates one class of exceptions to condition (A): conjoined NPs constitute one class of exceptions at least for the quantifier *both*:

(11) a. I found John and Mary, both.
b. I visited London and Paris, both.
c. *I found John and Mary and Susan, all.
d. *I visited the capitals of the world, all.

The contrast between (11a, b) and (11c, d) shows that the exception is restricted to *both*, which seems to be curious. This curiosity calls for explanation.

Maling posits subcondition (B) to the effect that Q-Floating can apply only if the "following phrase" can reasonably be associated (semantically) with the NP that the quantifier binds:

(12) a. *I saw the men all yesterday.
b. *She found the missing books both/all quickly.
c. *He argued with the men all/each/both about politics.
d. *They went after the thieves both on bicycles.

These sentences satisfy condition (A): the floated quantifiers are followed by some constituent, "the following phrase". However, they violate subcondition (B); *the men* and *yesterday* in (12a), *the missing books* and *quickly* in (12b), *the men* and *about politics* in (12c), and *the thieves* and *on the bicycles* in (12d) do not have some semantic association, respectively.

Subcondition (B) is a reasonable one, which is one of the selectional restrictions.

Condition (A) must be modified not only by subcondition (B) but also by subcondition (C). There is a correlation between Q-Floating and Passive rule. Maling (1976) mentions that Visser (1973) observes that Passive rule is only possible when the complement relates to the immediately preceding NP. Thus, neither Passive nor Q-Floating may apply to the object NP if the "following phrase" relates to the subject:

(13) a. He considers his friends <u>all</u> (as) pompous.
b. *He impressed his friends <u>all</u> as pompous.
c. His friends are (all) considered by him as pompous.
d. *His friends were (all) impressed by him as pompous.

(14) a. Mary made the boys <u>all</u> (into) good little housekeepers.
b. *Mary made the boys <u>all</u> a good mother.
c. The boys were (all) made good little housekeepers by Mary.
d. *The boys were (all) made a good mother by Mary.

(15) a. Frank persuaded the men <u>all</u> to leave.
b. *Frank promised the men <u>all</u> to leave.
c. The men were (all) persuaded to leave by Frank.
d. *The men were (all) promised to leave by Frank.

Compare (a) and (b) versions. The (a) versions are grammatical because the "following phrases" relate to Q-floated objects, whereas the (b) versions are not grammatical, because the "following phrases" relate to the subjects. This contrast is also reflected in the passive sentences, (c) and (d) versions.

Note that the (b) versions above become grammatical if the object NPs are not Q-floated:

(16) a. He impressed all of his friends as pompous. (cf. 13b)
b. Mary made all of the boys a good mother. (cf. 14b)
c. Frank promised all of the men to leave. (cf. 15b)

The contrast between the ungrammatical (b) versions in (13–15) and the grammatical versions in (16) hinges on whether or not Q-Floating has applied. This is just a superficial observation. There must be some semantic reason: the sequence of "NP-Q" has the "following phrase" in its scope, while the sequence of "Q-NP" may or may not have the "following phrase" in its scope. The scope-bearing element has influence/power on the element in its scope (cf. Yang 1993e). Thus, Q-Floating emphasizes quantifiers. This view can solve the thus far unexplored question why the so-called "following phrase" is required in the process of Quantifier Floating (=condition A). My answer is quite simple but intuitively appealing: if the "following phrase" is lacking, the floated quantifier has nothing in its scope/power. If nothing is to be affected, why does the speaker have to bother to move some specific element to the end of the sentence? This explanation can subsume all the conditions and constraints involved in Q-Floating. One might raise the objection to the effect that my explanation cannot accomodate the exceptions in (11). My answer to this objection is this: the conjoined NPs can be more strongly bound by the floated quantifiers. That is, the speaker floats the quantifier in order to strongly bind the conjoined NPs. This explanation, however, is not perfectly appealing intuitively, because *both* and *all* behave differently. That is, the question remains why *both* can strongly bind conjoined NPs, while *all* cannot.

Exercises and problems

1. What is the function of Quantifier Floating?
2. Why is the "following phrase" required in Q-Floating?
3. Why is it that Q-Floating can apply to conjoined NPs without the "following phrase", in the case of both?
4. How is the notion of "scope" involved in Q-Floating?
5. Why is it that the floated quantifier tends to have the "following phrase" in its scope?
6. Is there any significant meaning difference between (a) and (b)? What number does *some* refer to in (a)? Put (a) into your mother tongue.
   a. Some speakers do not accept that sentence.
   b. There are speakers who do not accept that sentence.

Unit 19

Raising-to-Object and Raising-to-Subject

The subject of a lower clause may be raised to the object position of the higher clause. The rule is called Raising-to-Object. Whether this rule must be admitted or not is controversial. I proceed on the assumption that this rule must be admitted, especially for pedagogical purposes (i.e. alternative expressibility).

The following illustrate the rule:

(1) a. They expected that John would solve the problem.
    b. They expected John to solve the problem.
    c. John was expected by them to solve the problem.(passive)

(2) a. John considered that Mary was innocent.
    b. John considered Mary to be innocent.
    c. Mary was considered to be innocent.

(3) a. We know that the lady is the prime minister of England.
    b. We know the lady to be the prime minister of England.
    c. The lady is known to be the prime minister of England.

(4) a. We can depend on it that their paper will expose crooked politicians.
    b. We can depend on their paper to expose crooked politicians.
    c. ?Their paper can be depended on by us to expose crooked politicians.

(5) a. John believes that there is a trouble between them.
b. John believes there to be a trouble between them.
c. *There is believed by John to be a trouble between them.

In the (a) sentences, the underlined words are subjects of the lower clauses. In the (b) sentences, the same underlined words are objects of the higher clauses. In this sense, the subject of the lower clause is said to be raised to the object position in the higher clause. The (c) sentences are derived from the (b) sentences by Passive rule. The reason that (4c) is marginal is not known to me. The ungrammaticality of (5c) is due to the word *there*, which cannot be the passive's subject.

The straightforward description/explanation is not necessarily available in many rules. The rule under consideration is not exceptional:

(6) a. ?/*John wants that his parents leave him a fortune.
b. John wants his parents to leave him a fortune.

In (6), the source sentence (6a) is problematic. Many speakers do not accept (6a): it is marginal at best. The problem here is not a serious one, though. Sentence (6a) shows that the verb *want* does not select (= subcategorize for) a sentential complement for its object. The verb *want* selects an infinitival complement for its object:

(7) a. John wants for his parents to leave him a fortune.
b. John wants his parents to leave him a fortune.

Sentence (7b = 6b) is derived from (7a) by Raising-to-Object, but not from (6a).

Different verbs select different complements for their objects. In the case of the verb *hope*, it selects either sentential complement or infinitival complement, but not gerundival complement:

(8) a. I hope that you will have a happy summer.
b. I hope for you to have a happy summer.
c. *I hope you to have a happy summer.
d. *I hope your having a happy summer.
e. I hope for your having a happy summer.

In (8), the problem is (8c), which might be thought to be derived from either (a) or (b). But the problem is solved by saying that *hope* does not allow Raising-to-Object. In general, factive verbs and some non-factive verbs do not allow Raising-to-Object (for factivity, see Kiparsky and Kiparsky 1970). Compare (8d) and (8e). Sentence (8d) is not grammatical, because the verb *hope* does not select gerundival complement for its object. Sentence (8e) is possible because the verb *hope* must take *for* if the object is a noun (cf. Brame 1980), like *look for, search for, call for*, etc.

(9) a. *I hope it/rain/a miracle.
b. I hope for it/rain/a miracle.

Consider the following:

(10) a. John regrets that <u>Bacon</u> is the real author. (Cf. Baconian theory)
b. *John regrets <u>Bacon</u> to be the real author.

(11) a. The landlord demands that <u>the tenant</u> (should)vacate the room in five days.
b. *The landlord demands <u>the tenant</u> to vacate the room in five days.

The ungrammaticality of the (b) sentences is due to the fact that factive verbs (e.g. *regret*) and demand verbs do not allow Raising-to-Object.

A rather recalcitrant case is the following:

(12) a. They say that syntax is easy.
b. *They say syntax to be easy.
c. Syntax is said to be easy.

Sentence (12b) shows that the verb *say* does not allow Raising-to-Object. Then, what is the source of sentence (12c)? If (12b) is grammatical, no problem arises since it has the object. Since (12b) is not grammatical, (12c) cannot be derived from it. Then, an alternative source might be (12a). But it cannot be, because Passive rule requires the clause-mate condition. This means that only the object in the same clause with the subject can become the passive's subject. Thus, sentence (12c) is interesting as well as recalcitrant.

Let's try to remove recalcitrancy from sentence (12c). If "recalcitrancy" is removed from (12c), what remains in (12c) is "being interesting":

(13) a. People say that Kim is jealous of the girl.
b. That Kim is jealous of the girl is said. (by Passive)
c. It is said that Kim is jealous of the girl. (by Extra)
d. Kim is said to be jealous of the girl. (by Raising-to-Subject)

(13b) is derived from (13a) by Passive rule. This is possible because the whole sentential complement is the object of the main clause, that is, the subject and the object are clause mates. (13c) is derived from (13b) by Extra. Finally, (13d) is derived from (13c) by Raising-to-Subject. The same process can produce sentence (12c), which was regarded above as being "recalcitrant as well as interesting":

(14) a. They say that syntax is easy. (= 12a)
b. That syntax is easy is said. (by Passive)

c. It is said that syntax is easy. (by Extra)
d. Syntax is said to be easy. (by Raising-to-Subject) (= 12c)

This process will be specified later. Since the rule Raising-to-Subject is mentioned here, I will now specify the rule, and then return to Raising-to-Object.

Raising-to-Subject

Consider the following:

(15) a. That he will solve the problem is likely/unlikely.
b. It is likely/unlikely that he will solve the problem. (by Extra)
c. He is likely/unlikely to solve the problem.

(16) a. It seemed/happened/appeared/turned out that John fell in love with Susan.
b. John seemed/happened/appeared/turned out to have fallen in love with Susan.

Sentence (15c) is derived from (15b) by Raising-to-Subject. The subject of the lower clause/sentence is raised to the subject position of the higher clause/sentence. The same process yields (16b). It has been known that this rule is very restrictive in that the verbs are limited to *likely, unlikely, sure, certain, seem, happen, appear, turn out,* etc.

Now I would like to propose something new. Raising-to-Subject can also apply to the source structure (17a):

(17) a. Source: *It* - passive - *that* [subject - verb - . . .].
b. Result: Subject - passive - *to* verb . . .

The following illustrate the process in (17):

(18) a. It is said/rumored/alleged that John teaches magic.
b. John is said/rumored/alleged to teach magic.

This process can account for the derivation of (14d) from (14c).

How do we know that the subject of the lower clause is raised to the subject position of the higher clause? The answer is very simple: it is visible. What else is necessary to justify it?

We can show all the cases where Raising-to-Subject can apply:

(19) Source: *It* – *be likely* adj – *that* [subject – verb . . .]
– *seem* verb –
– passive –

Result: Subject – *be likely* adj – *to* – verb . . .
– *seem* verb –
– passive –

Now returning to Raising-to-Object, the justification is not so simple. Because the phrase which is claimed to be raised has the Janus status, that is, the phrase looks to belong to the preceding part, or to the following part, we are required to justify that the phrase in question belongs to the preceding part. Postal (1974:40–43) provides the following justifications:

By Passivization

(20) a. Mary believes that John works slow and steady.
b. That John works slow and steady is believed by Mary.
c. *John is believed by Mary that works slow and steady.

(21) a. Mary believes that <u>John</u> works slow and steady.
b. Mary believes <u>John</u> to work slow and steady.

c. *(For) John to work slow and steady is believed by Mary.
d. John is believed (by Mary) to work slow and steady.

(20) shows that Passive rule is subject to the "clause mate condition", which means that the subject and the object must be in the same clause. In (20a), the subject and the whole sentential complement object are in the same clause; that is, they are clause mates. Hence, (20b) is grammatical. In (20c), the subject is extracted from the different lower clause by getting over the clause boundary. Hence, it is not grammatical. Suppose that (21b) is derived from (21a) by Raising-to-Object. The ungrammaticality of (21c) shows that the raised word and the rest on the one hand and the subject on the other are not clause mates. (21d) is derived from (21b) by Passive rule. The subject in (21d) is from (21b). It is proved that Mary and John are clause mates in (21b). It is proved, in turn, that the subject *John* in (21a) is raised to the object position in (21b).

By Reflexivization

(22) a. John believed that he was immortal.
b. *John believed that himself was immortal.
c. John believed himself to be immortal.
d. *John_i believed him_i to be immortal.

Suppose the underlined words in each sentence are coreferential. The contrast between (22a) and (22b) shows that reflexivization is also subject to the clause mate condition. The contrast of (22c) and (22d) shows that *himself* and the subject in (22c) are clause mates. Hence, it is proved that the subject *he* in the lower clause in (22a) is raised to the object (*himself*) position in (22c).

By Reciprocal marking

(23) a. *They believed that each other were honest.
b. They believed each other to be honest.

In (22a), the coreferential words are not clause mates, which shows that reciprocal marking is also subject to the clause mate condition. The fact that (23b) is grammatical shows that *each other* and the subject are clause mates. Hence, it proves that the subject *each other* in the lower clause in (23a) is raised to the object position in (23b). So far, the justifications hinge on the clause mate condition.

By Complex NP Shift

(24) a. I showed all of the coffee grounds and lettuce cookies to John.
b. I showed (to) John all of the coffee grounds and lettuce cookies

(25) a. I think all of the men who recovered from mononucleosis are happy.
b. *I think are happy all of the men who recovered from mononucleosis.

(26) a. I believe that all of the gang members who were caught were innocent.
b. I believe all of the gang members who were caught to have been innocent.
c. I believe to have been innocent all of the gang members who were caught.

The contrast of (24b) and (25b) shows that Heavy NP Shift applies only to objects (cf. Unit 12). Suppose that (26b) is derived from (26a) by Raising-to-Object. (26c) is derived from (26b) by Heavy NP Shift. This proves that the shifted part in (26c) was the object in (26b), which in turn proves that the part was raised from the subject in (26a).

Here, I would like to stop echoing Postal's data and justifications, and add Rosenbaum's (1967:66–67) data and my justification:

(27) a. I want very much for you to go.
b. *I want for you to go very much.
c. *I want very much you to go.
d. I want you to go very much.

In (27), the adverbial *very much* modifies the main verb *want*. (27a) is grammatical because the modifying adverbial and the modified verb are clause mates. Adverbials can be placed between the verb and the complement object, but not between the verb and the noun object (cf. Unit 4). (27b) is not grammatical, because the adverbial and the verb are not clause mates, so that the adverbial modifies the verb in the infinitival complement. Notice that the grammaticality of the pair (27a) and (27b) is reversed in the pair (27c) and (27d). Sentence (27c) is not grammatical, because the adverbial is placed between the verb and the noun object *you*, which means that the adverbial and the verb are clause mates. Sentence (27d) is grammatical because the adverbial and the verb are clause mates. Thus, it is proved that the subject *you* of the lower clause (= infinitival complement) in (27a) and (27b) is raised to the object position of the higher clause (= the main clause) in (27c) and (27d). The examples in (27) cannot be accounted for without invoking Raising-to-Object.

Exercises and problems

1. It is arguable whether the italicized word in (b) is raised or not. Justify your position.
    a. John believes that Mary is honest.
    b. John believes *Mary* to be honest.

2. Classify verbs which allow Raising-to-Object, and which block it. Do the same thing with regard to Raising-to-Subject.
3. What is the meaning difference of "verb" and "verb *for*"?
4. What is the meaning difference of the following (a) and (b)? If there is some meaning difference, what is the cause of it?
    a. I expect that John will come to the party on time.
    b. I expect John to come to the party on time.
5. Discuss whether *I* and *you* are clause mates in the following.
    I want for you to study hard.
6. What are the syntactic and semantic difference of the following?
    a. I want for you to study music.
    b. I want you to study music.

Unit 20
Negative Raising

A negative which is in the subordinate (= lower) clause may be raised to the main (= higher) clause. This rule is also known as *Not*-Hopping or Negative Transportation. The following illustrate the rule:

(1) a. I believe that John does <u>not</u> discriminate races.
    b. I do <u>not</u> believe that John discriminates races.

George Lakoff (1970:148) observes that sentence (1b) is ambiguous: (i) the committal reading (= 1a) and (ii) the non-committal reading (= does not commit the speaker to any belief at all). The non-committal reading is possible only with language-sensitive speakers. Native speakers of English in general have only the committal reading, so that sentence (1a) and sentence (1b) are cognitively synonymous. Native speakers seem to prefer the neg-raised version.

On Negative Raising, opinions are divided. Some scholars claim that Negative Raising exists, and some others claim that the rule does not exist. Robin Lakoff (1969) provides evidence for Negative Raising, by means of Tag Questions and negative polarity items (NPIs).

By Tag Questions

(2) a. I think John doesn't like snakes, does he?
    b. I don't think John likes snakes, does he?
    c. *I don't think John likes snakes, doesn't he?

The tag question is not used for the speaker himself, simply because it is ridiculous to ask himself about his utterance. Of course, there are marked cases in which the speaker asks the addressee about the speaker himself. The tag question usually works on the basis of contrasting polarity. If the main (= host) clause is affirmative, the tag clause takes a negative form, and vice versa. In (2a), the subordinate clause (= sentential complement) of the host clause is negative, and the tag clause is affirmative. Hence, the whole sentence (2a) is grammatical. Sentence (2c) satisfies the above requirement, but it is not grammatical. This shows that the subordinate clause of the host clause is negative, although it contains no negative. This suggests that the negative in the subordinate clause is raised to the main clause, after Tag Question Formation has applied. This suggestion is supported by sentence (2b). Here, although the subordinate clause of the host clause is affirmative, the affirmative tag clause works. This justifies that the negative of the subordinate clause of the host clause existed when Tag Question Formation applied, and then the negative was raised.

Contra Robin Lakoff, Cattell (1973) argues that R. Lakoff's argument does not work, because tag questions have two forms: the contrasting polarity tag, and the matching tag:

(3) The book is obscene, isn't it? (Contrasting polarity tag)

(4) The book is obscene, is it? (Matching tag)

Matching tag means that the host clause is not put forward as the point of view of the speaker, but as possibly that of the listener. In contrast, contrasting polarity tag means that the speaker seems to be offering his own opinion and asking for agreement. There is another difference. Contrasting tag can be attached only to statements:

(5) a. John drank beer, didn't he?
b. *Did John drink beer, didn't he?

Matching tag, in contrast, can be attached not only to statements but also to questions:

(6) a. John drank beer, did he?
b. Did John drink beer, did he?

Thus, Cattell claims that R. Lakoff's argument for Neg Raising based on the tag question does not hold. For details, see Cattell (1973).

Robin Lakoff's another argument for Negative Raising is based on the negative polarity items:

(7) a. I believed that John wouldn't leave until tomorrow.
b. I didn't believe that John would leave until tomorrow.

(8) a. I claimed that John wouldn't leave until tomorrow.
b. *I didn't claim that John would leave until tomorrow.

In order to explain these data, we must understand NPI first. There are certain lexical items which are used only in negative contexts. For a few examples,

(9) a. *leave until vs. not leave until
b. *lift a finger vs. not lift a finger
c. *can help ... -ing vs. can't help ... -ing

In (9a), *until* is a duration adverb. The verb *leave* is not a duration verb, but a verb which acts momentarily. Hence, *leave until* is not compatible. If *leave* is combined with *not*, *not leave* means *stay*, which is a duration verb. Hence, *not leave until* is compatible since it means *stay until*.

Returning to examples (7) and (8), sentence (7a) is grammatical because the negative polarity item is used in a negative context. In sentence (7b), the NPI is used in a positive context. Hence, (7b) is expected to be ungrammatical. Nonetheless, (7b) is grammatical. Why is it? If we assume that the negative exists in the main clause, although the NPI is in the subordinate clause, then we can account for the grammaticality of (7b). This assumption leads to evidence that the negative in the subordinate clause is raised to the main clause. Sentence (8a) is grammatical for the same reason as for (7a). Sentence (8b) has the same structure as (7b). But (8b) is not grammatical. The only difference between (7b) and (8b) is the difference of the main verbs: *believe* vs. *claim*.

Thus, verbs are divided into two classes: one class allows the Negative Raising, and the other class does not allow the rule. This distinction of verbs can explain the difference of (7b) and (8b). It is known that negative raising verbs are restricted to the following:

(10) a. Opinion verbs: *believe, think, suppose, predict, suggest, expect, see, imagine*, etc.
b. Intent verbs: *want, intend, plan, choose, desire* (= *want*), etc.

What is in common among the negative raising verbs seems to be more or less mental verbs. This, however, does not mean that all mental verbs allow negative raising. The exact specification calls for research.

An interesting question is: why certain mental verbs allow Neg Raising. A simple answer is: the two sentences in (11), where the verb *think* is involved, are cognitively and intuitively identical; while the two sentences in (12), where the verb *regret* is involved, are not identical. Thus, verbs like *think* allow Negative Raising, whereas verbs like *regret* block the rule.

(11) a. I think that he is not reliable.
b. I don't think that he is reliable. (= 11a)

(12) a. I regret that he is not reliable.
b. I don't regret that he is reliable.

With this simple answer, some readers will nod their heads, but others will shake their heads. This means that a more appealing explanation is called for.

Exercises and problems

1. What are two types of polarity items?
2. Explain why *leave until* is not possible, whereas *not leave until* is possible. And generalize this distinction.
3. There are pros and cons with respect to Negative Raising. Justify your position.
4. Provide some examples of negative polarity item in your mother tongue.
5. Specify the distinction of contrasting tag and matching tag.
6. On what basis, do statement, matching tag, contrasting tag, and question make a hierarchy?

Unit 21

Tough Movement

There are adjectives and nominals which express difficulty or easiness. The adjective *tough* represents this class of words. The following illustrate the rule:

(1) a. To get along with John is easy.
    b. It is easy to get along with John. (by Extra)
    c. John is easy to get along with.

(2) a. For them to persuade the dictator is difficult.
    b. It is difficult for them to persuade the dictator. (by Extra)
    c. The dictator is difficult for them to persuade.

(3) a. To talk to John was a delight.
    b. It was a delight to talk to John. (by Extra)
    c. John was a delight to talk to.

In these sentences, *Tough* Movement links (b) to (c). This rule moves the object (including the preposition's object) NP which is in the infinitival complement clause to the front of the sentence.

This rule works only with the following adjectives and nominals which occur in the [ ] slot of "*It* - *be* - [ ] - infinitive":

(4) a. Adjectives : *difficult, easy, hard, impossible, simple, tough*
    b. Nominals : *bitch* (= a hard time), *breeze* (= an easy time), *delight*, *gas* (= a lot of fun), *joy, pain in the neck/ass*

In the following, the (c) version is not grammatical:

(5) a. To please John is possible.
b. It is possible to please John. (by Extra)
c. *John is possible to please.

A serious question here is: why is it that *impossible* belongs to the class of *tough* predicates, whereas *possible* does not? This question is very natural and meaningful, in connection with the pair *difficult* and *easy*, which are *tough* predicates. One might regard *possible* as an exception. However, there is a very simple answer, whatever theories claim. The *tough* predicates in (4) mean either difficulty or easiness. *Impossible* means difficulty; hence, it belongs to the *tough* class. However, *possible* does not mean easiness; it means either easy or difficult. A *tough* predicate is required to be one of easiness and difficulty, but not both. This is the reason that *possible* is not a *tough* predicate. That is, *possible* is a category outsider of *tough* predicates. This is also the reason that "*tough* predicates" are also referred to as "*easy* predicates".

Consider the following:

(6) a. It is easy to seduce an idle girl.
b. *An idle girl is easy to seduce.

(7) a. It is difficult to kill someone with this gun.
b. *Someone is difficult to kill with this gun.

These examples show that indefinite NPs cannot be fronted in the *tough*-moved sentence. This restriction is also not groundless. Indefinite NPs cannot be judged either easy or difficult. This semantic/pragmatic property of indefinite NPs explains the restiction on indefinite NPs. However, generic expressions in the indefinite form (a generic sentence takes bare plural, definite, or indefinite noun) can be fronted:

(8) a. It is difficult to domesticate a tiger.
    b. A tiger is difficult to domesticate.

A tiger in these sentences does not mean either a specific tiger or a non-specific tiger, but tigers in general. We can easily judge that it is difficult to domesticate tigers. Sentence (8b) shows that what is important is not only the form but also the meaning. Sentence (8b) is grammatical only in the sense that *a tiger* is a generic expression.

Lasnik and Fiengo (1974) present predicates similar to, but different from, *tough* predicates:

(9) a. Mary is pretty to look at.
    b. *It is pretty to look at Mary.

(10) a. This flower is fragrant to smell.
     b. *It is fragrant to smell this flower.

(11) a. That music is melodious to listen to.
     b. *It is melodious to listen to that music.

(12) a. Mary is graceful to dance with.
     b. *It is graceful to dance with Mary.

Suppose that the predicates in these sentences are *tough* predicates. Then, a problem arises: their source sentences, the (b) versions, are not grammatical, against our natural expectation. This difference from *tough* predicate constructions is not accidental: the predicates belong to a different class, which includes nominals as well:

(13) a. This room is a pigsty to behold

b. *It is a pigsty to behold this room.

(14) a. The Columbia was a marvel to watch.
b. *It was a marvel to watch the Columbia.

(15) a. This problem is a hornet's nest to deal with.
b. *It is a hornet's nest to deal with this problem.

The ungrammaticality of (b) versions in (9) through (15) is due to the mismatch between the predicator and the predicatee. For instance, it is natural to say *Mary is pretty*; whereas it is not natural to say *To look at Mary is pretty*. This property is different from the case of *tough* predicates. It is natural to say *To seduce Mary is difficult*; whereas it is not natural to say *Mary is difficult*.

Since the predicates in (9-15) are different from *tough* predicates, Lasnik and Fiengo set up a different class of predicates, which are referred to as "Pure Object Deletion predicates":

(16) a. Aadjectives: *pretty, delicious, fragrant, graceful, melodious, tasty, beautiful, scratchy, pungent* (= *acrid*)
b. Nominals: *hornet's nest, pigsty, loony bin, bastard, tyrant, angel, prince, marvel*

The term "pure object deletion" is used for the following reason:

(17) a. *Mary is pretty to look at Mary. (the source of b)
b. Mary is pretty to look at [e].

(17b) is derived from (17a) by Pure Object Deletion.

The two classes of predicates, *Tough*-predicates and Pure-object- deletion-predicates (T-predicates, D-predicates, respectively) are different:

(18) a. T-predicates: are used for the description of action/activity.
b. D-predicates: are used for the description of objects.

(19) a. T-predicates: denote an objective experience.
b. D-predicates: denote a subjective evaluation.

(20) a. T-predicates: *John is easy. John is easy to please.
b. D-predicates: Sue is pretty. Sue is pretty to look at.

Concerning (19b), objective adjectives are not used for D-predicate constructions. The underlined adjectives below are objective ones. Hence, the following sentences are not grammatical:

(21) a. *This room is rectangular to live in.
b. *Coal is black to look at.

The subject (= *for* NP) of infinitival complement is not used for D-predicate constructions. This is due to the fact that somebody cannot do somebody else's subjective evaluation (except for the case where somebody authoritatively does somebody else's subjective evaluation-subjectivization of objective view point):

(22) a. ??Sue is pretty for Bill to look at.
b. ??This room is a pigsty for Sam to live in.

In these sentences, the speaker does others' (= the underlined ones) subjective evaluation, which results in marginality. The reason that they are not completely ungrammatical is due to the speaker's subjectivization of others' view point.

Concerning (20), in (20a), the underlined part (= infinitival complement) is required: otherwise, the information of the main clause is not sufficient.

In (20b), the underlined part is redundant because the predication of the main clause presupposes the underlined part.

Returning to (16b), nouns of D-predicates are metaphorical:

(23) a. This paint is like concrete to work with.
     b. *This paint is concrete to work with.

(24) a. This coffee is like tar to drink.
     b. *This coffee is tar to drink.

(25) a. John is like Nixon to talk to.
     b. *John is Nixon to talk to.

Lasnik and Fiengo provide these examples in order to show that nouns in the D-predicate class are metaphorically used. The (a) sentences are grammatical because the underlined parts (= *like* + concrete noun) are metaphorically used. The (b) sentences are not grammatical, because the nouns without *like* are not metaphorical. However, it seems to me that the (b) sentences can also be used metaphorically. If my judgment is not correct, that is the reflection of one of differences between Korean and English.

Nanni's (1980) work on this subject also deserves our attention. She claims that the "adjective + infinitive" sequence in *tough*-moved sentences can function as a single constituent:

(26) a. How hard to understand is Yang's humor book?
     b. How simple to persuade were the students?
     c. How difficult to solve was the problem?

(27) a. John certainly is, and Mary may well be, easy to tease.
     b. The law boards may be, and the CPA exam definitely was, hard to pass.

c. War and Peace may have been, but 'conditions on transformations' certainly was, tough to read.

(28) a. How easy to tease John is!
b. How difficult to study for the final exam was!
c. How simple to understand his speech was!

The "adjective + infinitive" sequence behaves as a single constituent, which is shown through WH-movement (26), Right Node Raising (27) (which will be dealt with in Unit 23), and Exclamation (28).

For some speakers, the gap which results from *Tough* Movement can occur at an unbounded distance from the adjective:

(29) a. It was difficult to persuade Bill to wear the coat.
b. The coat was difficult to persuade Bill to wear [e].

(30) a. It was hard to convince John to marry the girl.
b. The girl was hard to convince John to marry [e].

(31) a. It was easy to try to finish the assignment before noon.
b. The assignment was easy to try to finish [e] before noon.

(32) a. It was tough to attempt to climb the mountain.
b. The mountain was tough to attempt to climb [e].

In the (b) sentences, there are more than one infinitive between the adjective and the gap (marked by [e]). Let us test whether the string of "adjective + more than a single infinitive" behaves like the string of "adjective + a single infinitive", which is a single constituent (cf. 26–28):

(33) a. *How difficult to persuade Bill to wear was the coat?
b. *How hard to convince John to marry was the girl?

c. *We didn't know how easy to try to finish the assignment was.
d. *We asked how tough to attempt to climb the mountain was.

We see, through examples (26–28), that the sequence of "adjective + a single infinitive" behaves as a single constituent. However, the sequence of "adjective + more than one infinitive" does not behave as a single constituent (cf. 33).

The subject (= *for* NP) of infinitival complement may occur between adjective and infinitive:

(34) a. John is easy for the children to tease.
b. The girl was simple for Bill to fool.
c. The problem was difficult for us to avoid.

The sequence of "adj + *for-to* inf", however, does not behave as a single constituent:

(35) a. *How easy for the children to tease is John?
b. *How simple for Bill to fool was the girl?
c. *How difficult for us to avoid was the problem?

Thus, we can summarize as follows:

(36) a. "Adjective + *to*-Infinitive": a single constituent
b. "Adjective + more than one *to*-Infinitive": not a single constituent
c. "Adjective + *for-to*-Infinitive": not a single constituent

On the basis of the above findings, Nanni claims that the sequence of "Adj + a single Inf" is a "complex adjective". This claim is justified by its prenominal occurrence:

(37) a. an easy-to-take laxative

b. rare and hard-to-find manuscripts
c. a tough-to-please boss
d. a simple-to-solve problem
e. difficult-to-sit babies, etc.

Nanni's "complex adjectives" are subject to a few constraints: (i) they do not undergo adverb formation with *-ly*, and (ii) the degree word *enough* does not follow complex adjectives, unlike usual cases (cf. Sadler and Arnold 1994:212-3):

(38) a. easy → easily
b. easy-to-solve → *easy-to-solvely

(39) a. hard enough to pronounce
b. *hard-to-pronounce enough

Exercises and problems

1. Why is it that *impossible* belongs to the *tough*-predicate class, while *possible* does not?
2. How can we distinguish between *tough* predicates and pure-object-deletion predicates?
3. Translate a *tough* predicate sentence and a pure object deletion predicate sentence into your mother tongue. What is the difference of the two translated versions?
4. Why is it that indefinite NPs cannot be moved to the front in the *tough*-moved sentence?
5. In what context can indefinite NPs be moved to the front in the

tough-moved sentence?

6. Discuss whether the sequence of "*tough* adjective + a single infinitive" is a single constituent.
7. Can the sequence of "*tough* adjective + a single infinitive" occur prenominally?
8. Is the following adverb formation possible?

   easy-to-type → easily-to-type

9. Arrange the words in the parentheses, so that it makes sense in the context. What are all the possible alternatives?

   Could I ever learn about life and peace? To me, with my vast ignorance, it (achieve, impossible, a/an, seemed, task, to).

10. Are the following sentences (a) and (b) conjoinable like (c)? If not, why?

    (1) a. John is easy to persuade.
        b. Mary is pretty to look at.
        c. John is easy to persuade and Mary is pretty to look at.
    (2) a. To drink coffee is unhealthy.
        b. Smoking cigarettes is unhealthy.
        c. To drink coffee and smoking cigarettes are unhealthy.
    (3) a. John broke the window.
        b. A hammer broke the window.
        c. John and a hammer broke the window.

Unit 22

Complement Preposing

One of complex sentences has the form: "Subject + Verb + Sentential Complement Object". There are cases, in which the sentential complement object is placed to the front of the whole sentence. Hence, this rule is called Complement Preposing (Hooper 1975). This rule is also known as Complement Fronting (Emonds 1976), or Slifting (Ross 1973). By this rule, the main clause is downgraded, and the subordinate clause (= sentential complement) is highlighted. The rule is illustrated below:

(1) a. I think that John is a gay.
b. John is a gay, I think.
c. John is, I think, a gay.

(2) a. I believe that we must continue to show our filial piety to our parents.
b. We must continue to show our filial piety to our parents, I believe.

(3) a. He suspects that the boss is insane beyond all hope.
b. The boss is insane, he suspects, beyond all hope.

If the main clause is negative, the preposed subordinate clause must also be negative:

(4) a. I don't expect that John is coming today.
b. John isn't coming today, I don't expect.

(5) a. I don't think that Mary knows how to behave.
b. Mary doesn't know how to behave, I don't think.

(6) a. I don't believe that those facts can be explained.
b. Those facts can't be explained, I don't believe.

This requirement is not accidental. Suppose the preposed subordinate clause is not negative. Then, the speaker contradicts himself because the already negated subordinate clause becomes affirmative. In order to avoid such contradiction, both clauses must be negative.

Similarly, in questions, both clauses must be questioned:

(7) a. Do you think that John is a gay?
b. Is John a gay, do you think?

(8) a. Do you suppose that you can help me?
b. Can you help me, do you suppose?

(9) a. Do you expect that you have enough gas to get to Boston?
b. Do you have enough gas to get to Boston, do you expect?

This requirement is not accidental. If the preposed subordinate clause is not questioned, it follows that the speaker presupposes that he has no question about the subordinate clause. This presupposition conflicts with the sentence's question. In order to avoid this conflict, the preposed subordinate clause must also be questioned. For example,

(8') a. Do you suppose that you can help me?
b. *<u>You can help me</u>, do you suppose?
c. Can you help me, do you suppose?

In (8'b), the underlined preposed subordinate clause is affirmative. That is, the speaker presupposes that "you can help me". And then, the same speaker asks about his presupposed statement. Thus, the preposed clause and the downgraded clause are contradictory. In order to avoid such contradiction, both clauses must be questioned, as in (8'c).

These explanations are "intuitively appealing" ones. Technically speaking, the subordinate clause which was in the scope of negative or question of the main clause cannot be extracted with no reason. The reason that the preposed subordinate clause must accord with the degraded main clause (i.e. negated or questioned) is this: once X is in Y's scope, X must carry its mark that it was in Y's scope wherever it is. Otherwise, the original meaning/function is changed.

Naturally, negative sentential verbs block the rule:

(10) a. I deny that Sue had a baby before marriage.
b. *Sue had a baby before marriage, I deny.

(11) a. We forgot that yesterday was Susan's birthday.
b. *Yesterday was Susan's birthday, we forgot.

(12) a. I doubt that Kim is generous.
b. *Kim is generous, I doubt.

(13) a. I don't think that Bill is a chauvinist.
b. *Bill is, I don't think, a chauvinist.

The reason was provided above that the (b) versions, where complements are preposed, are not grammatical.

Next, consider the following:

(14) a. I don't deny that eating onions may help our health.
b. Eating onions may, I don't deny, help our health.

(15) a. I don't doubt that eating kimchi prevents cancer.
b. Eating kimchi prevents cancer, I don't doubt.

In the (b) versions, where complements are preposed, the preposed clauses are not negative, although the downgraded main clauses are negative. But they are grammatical. The reason is very simple: the double negation means affirmative (e.g. not deny → agree, not doubt → believe). This fact also suggests that semantic factors must be evoked, if necessary, in syntactic analysis/understanding.

In the process of complement preposing, as mentioned above, the complement clause is highlighted, while the main clause is downgraded. That is, the main clause is parentheticalized: the downgraded main clause is a parenthetical clause. In most cases, the parenthetical clause may have the *as*-clause counterpart:

(16) a. I expected that John returned on Saturday.
b. John returned on Saturday, I expected.
c. John returned on Saturday, as I expected.

(17) a. I thought that John returned today.
b. John returned today, I thought. (returning first, thinking next)
c. John returned today, as I thought. (thinking first, returning next)

(18) a. I think that Sue came today.
b. Sue came today, I think.
c. *Sue came today, as I think.

In (16) and (17), the (b) versions and the (c) versions are quite similar in meaning. One difference is that of the time sequence, as indicated in (17). Sentence (18c) is not grammatical, which is due to the mismatch of the time sequence.

Main verbs determine whether complement preposing is allowed or blocked. This calls for classification of verbs. Figuratively speaking, if the main clause is strong enough to defend itself, the subordinate clause cannot pull the main clause down. This power hinges on the main verb. For example, demand and request verbs may occur in *as*-clauses, but not in parentheticals:

(19) a. I demanded/requested that John come today.
b. John came today, as I demanded/requested.
c. *John came today, I demanded/requested.

Sentence (19c) is not grammatical, because the main verbs are strong enough to reject being downgraded.

The effect of Complement Preposing is to make the complement proposition (= the subordinate clause) the main assertion of the sentence, while reducing the original main clause to parenthetical or secondary status. On the basis of the effect of Complement Preposing, Hooper (1975) classifies verbs into "Assertives" and "Non-assertives":

(20) a. Assertives: allow Complement Preposing
b. Non-assertives: block Complement Preposing

The distinction of assertives and non-assertives is rather confusing. What Hooper intends to assert is that the speaker gives assertiveness to the complement clause, not to the main clause. This is the cause that the verb *assert* itself belongs to the class of non-assertives. For further details, see Hooper (1975).

Exercises and problems

1. What is the function of Complement Preposing?
2. Why is it that a negative in the main clause blocks the rule?
3. Why is it that demand and request verbs block the rule?
4. Is the verb *assert* an assertive or a non-assertive? Why?
5. Why is it that *not deny/doubt* do not block the rule?
6. Why is it that, in questions, both clauses must be questioned in the complement preposed sentence?
7. Compare parenthetical clauses and *as*-clauses.
8. Is assertivity relevant to other rules?
9. What is the relation between factivity and assertivity?

Unit 23

Right Node Raising

The terms "right/left node" and "right node raising" are technical ones, connected with the tree diagram. For the understanding of the rule "Right Node Raising" (RNR, for short), we can do without such technicality. Suppose two clauses have the same expressions placed toward the right sides of the clauses. In cases like this, we can chop the shared expression of each clause, and put it at the end of the whole sentence. The chopped site of each clause (= conjunct) is marked by dashes or a comma. Thus, RNR is one of the economizing devices.

The following illustrate the rule:

(1) a. Tom may be a fox and Tony certainly is a fox.
    b. Tom may be–and Tony certainly is–a fox.
    c. Tom may be, and Tony certainly is, a fox. (= b)

(2) a. John said he would smoke pot and Bill actually smoked pot.
    b. John said he would, and Bill actually did, smoke pot.

(3) a. John said he would eat such meat and Bill actually ate such meat.
    b. John said he would, and Bill actually did, eat such meat.

(4) a. Harry claims that Sam is a lunatic but nobody has so far proved that Sam is a lunatic.
    b. Harry claims, but nobody has so far proved, that Sam is a lunatic.

In (2a), the same/shared expression is *pot* since *smoke* and *smoked* have slightly different forms. However, if we analyze *smoked* as *did smoke*, the same/shared expression becomes larger like *smoke pot*. This is realized in (2b). The same thing has taken place in (3). This adjustment is not an arbitrary one, but a maximizing device of economy.

Conjuncts in RNR take not only clausal forms but also sub-clausal forms:

(5) a. Doctors are sometimes very good at giving, as well as asking for, money. (Johnson (ed.) 1989. *A Treasury of Humor*. p. 190)
b. A speaker is absolved of any responsibility for, or commitment to, any aspect of what he mentions. (*JL* 25:119)
c. Such non-presuppositional theories thereby entirely fail to predict that, let alone explain why, the examples in Set 1 do, as a matter of empirical fact, fall together with . . . (*JL* 25:120)

In (5), RNRs have applied to sub-clauses.

In the 1970s, some scholars discussed about constituency in conjunction with RNR. Bresnan (1974:615) argues that RNR is a sufficient, but not a necessary, condition for constituency. In other words, if a string undergoes RNR, it must be a constituent, but not conversely:

(6) He tried to persuade {the students, them} that he was right, but he couldn't convince {the students, them} that he was right..

(7) a. He tried to persuade them, but he couldn't convince them, <u>that he was right</u>.
b. *He tried to persuade, but he couldn't convince, <u>them that he was right</u>.
c. *He tried to persuade, but he couldn't convince, <u>the students that he was right</u>.

(8) a. He tried to persuade, but he couldn't convince, the students he liked.

b. *He tried to persuade, but he couldn't convince, them.

If we apply RNR to (6), it yields (7). Sentence (7a) is grammatical because the underlined part is a constituent. In contrast, (7b, c) are not grammatical, because the underlined parts are not constituents.

Abbott (1976:639–642) summarizes some authors' claims:

(9) a. Bresnan (1974:615): the ability of a string to undergo RNR is a sufficient, if not a necessary, condition for constituenthood.

b. Postal (1974:125–128): uses this criterion as a test in establishing nonconstituenthood.

c. Hankamer (1971:ch. 1): only, if not all, constituents may undergo RNR.

d. Abbott (1976:639–642): RNR sentences cannot be used uncritically as tests for constituent structure.

Abbott claims that the following data are inconsistent with any claim on a single constituent:

(10) Smith loaned, and his widow later donated, a valuable collection of manuscripts to the library.

(11) I borrowed, and my sister stole, large sums of money from the Chase Manhattan Bank.

(12) Leslie played, and Mary sang, some of C & W songs at George's party.

(13) Mary baked, and George frosted, 20 cakes in less than an hour.

It is clear that each of the underlined parts (= RNRed elements) is not a single constituent.

Hankamer (1971:76) judges that the following are not grammatical:

(14) a. *John offered, and Harry gave, Sally a Cadillac.
b. *John asserted, and Harry denied, to Seymour that Sally was a virgin.
c. *John told, and Harry showed, Seymour that Sally was a virgin.
d. *Chomsky asserted, and McCawley denied, that a level of "deep structure" existed at the semantics conference.

Abbott comments, as follows, on Hankamer's judgments: (14a) may be improved by transposing DO and IO as in *John offered, and Harry gave, a Cadillac to Sally.* (14b) is ungrammatical because of the ungrammaticality of **Harry denied to Seymour that Sally was a virgin.* (14c) has the same structure as the following, which is almost perfectly grammatical: ?*John tried to persuade, but failed to convince, his skeptical examiners that he knows the right answers.* And (14d) is grammatical, especially with a pause after *existed.*

Abbott contends that the claim that the ability to undergo RNR is a necessary condition for constituenthood appears to be somewhat more reliable. The only contrary example is Bresnan's example (8b). However, the ungrammaticality of (8b) may be due to the fact that it strands a relatively uninformative pronoun *them* in a position of prominence, just as:

(15) a. *He called up her. (cf. He called her up.)
b. *I gave Sally it. (cf. I gave it to Sally.)

She hypothesizes that the relative ungrammaticality of some RNR sentences is not so much a result of constituent structure, but is caused instead by factors that make processing difficult or that produce clumsy and stylistically inappropriate examples. Among such factors are:

(16) a. Relative "lightness" or unimportance of raised material,
b. Slightly different role relations of a stranded NP to the conjoined verbs, and
c. Stranded NP–NP sequence may also contribute to ungrammaticality.

It seems to me that another important factor to be considered is dialectal and/or idiolectal variation. This factor cannot be ignored, because eminent scholars' judgments are not necessarily the same.

Exercises and problems

1. Why is RNR necessary?
2. Provide some examples where RNR has applied to sub-clauses.
3. Is the raised material limited to a single constituent?
4. There are other "economizing devices". Specify them.
5. Describe the necessary and sufficient condition.
6. What is the "End-weight Maxim"? How is this notion related to RNRed sentences?
7. Discuss whether RNR is involved in the following:

   Most – indeed all – of the authors I have read on the subject of metaphor assume that we know how literal utterances work . . .

Unit 24

Special Passives

Learners of English as a second/foreign language may think that they know how to convert actives and passives. However, when it comes to "special passives", such an assumption does not necessarily hold. Here I deal with (i) "middle" verb constructions, (ii) "peculiar" passives, (iii) activo-passives, and (iv) *un*-passives.

Middle Verb Constructions

What I call middle verb constructions refer to the active constructions which lack their corresponding passives. The term "middle" is currently confusing because some authors (e.g. Lees 1960, Keyser & Roeper 1984, Fagan 1988, among others) have used the term in different ways. Their middles refer to what Jespersen (1927) called "activo-passives". The gap of passives here is due to the nature of verbs which can take objects. Middle verbs include the following:

(1) Middle verbs: *resemble, have, lack, cost, weigh, marry, suit, fit, strike, impress,* etc.

One might regard this restriction just as a syntactic exception to passivization. Nonetheless, this restriction hinges on some semantic properties of the active sentence. The passive, in general, requires the active to satisfy certain conditions. These requirements are referred to as Passive's Requirements of Active (for short, PRA) (cf. Yang 1999a). An active sentence cannot be passivized if it does not satisfy PRA. I posit PRA as follows:

(2) Passive's Requirements of Active (PRA)

a. Affection condition:
The subject of an active is required to affect/influence the object.

b. Agent subject condition:
The subject of an active is required to be an agent, which is an instigator, regardless of intentionality.

c. Patient object condition:
The object of an active is required to be a patient.

The affection relation requires an affector and an affectee; the former is the subject and the latter is the object of an active sentence. This condition excludes intransitive-verb constructions from being passivized. The agent subject condition follows, as a corollary, from the affection condition. This condition excludes non-agent subject constructions, typically "middle constructions", from being passivized. The patient object condition follows, also as a corollary, from the affection condition. This condition saves "peculiar" passives. Since the affection condition is the core condition, the PRA may alternatively be called the "affection hypothesis".

I contend that if an active does not satisfy PRA (= Affection Hypothesis), it cannot have its corresponding passive, as far as "middle constructions" and "peculiar passives" are concerned. Consider the following:

(3) a. John resembles Bill.
b. *Bill is resembled by John.

The resemblance of two entities is not a relation of affection: the subject is not an agent, and the object is not a patient. Hence, the active sentence (3a) cannot have its passive (3b). (3a) just describes some state, but not an action. Incidentally, *resemble* can take progressive:

(3) c. John is resembling his father day after day.

The following examples can also be explained by PRA:

(4) a. John has a good book.
b. *A good book is had by John.

The verb *have* means possession. Possession relates a locative subject and an unaffectable object. This means that the subject of (4a) is not an agent. Hence, the active sentence (4a) cannot have its passive (4b).

Have, possess, and *own* have similar, if not identical, cooccurrence and selectional restrictions, yet *own* may be passivized while *have* and *possess* may not. Dixon (1991:308–9) indicates the difference of them. *Have* differs from *own*: *have* refers to a general property of the owner, whereas *own* focuses on the possession and implies that the owner has a legal, or some other official, right to it. And *possess* differs from *own* in that *possess* implies a strong emotional or mental connection between the owner and the possession. To sum up, *own* implies that the owner has a legal, or some other official, right to the possession, whereas *have* and *possess* do not imply such a right. If this is true, we can say that the subject (= the owner) of the sentence whose verb is *own* has some influence/affection on the object (= the possession). Then, it follows that the subject of the sentence is an agent subject, which satisfies PRA. This is the reason that *own* may be passivized. The other two verbs lack the influence/affection property and may not be passivized.

Green (1974:3) notes that a passive form of *have* appears in only two expressions:

(5) a. A good time was had by all.
    b. Bill has been had by John.

She indicates that sentence (5a) is a facetious fixed expression and that the verb *have* in (5b) means *take in*. What is important to note here is that the verb *have* in (5a) is not a possession verb; it means *enjoy*. Enjoyment relates an agent subject and a patient object. Hence, the passive sentence (5a) is possible because PRA is satisfied. The verb *have* in (5b) is not a possession verb; it means *take in*. *Taking-in* relates an agent subject and a patient object. Hence, the passive sentence (5b) is also possible under PRA.

The active sentences in the following also lack their passives:

(6) a. The book costs ten dollars.
    b. *Ten dollars is cost by the book.

(7) a. The car weighs two tons.
    b. *Two tons is weighed by the car.

The verbs *cost* and *weigh* do not require agent subjects. The active sentences just describe some states, relating a non-agent subject and an object. Hence, the passive sentences above are not possible under PRA.

The following sentences are more interesting:

(8) a. Susan married John.
    b. *John was married by Susan.

(9) a. The suit fits me.
    b. *I am fitted by the suit.

In (8a), the subject might be an agent, although an atypical one. Then, the active sentence (8a) seems to satisfy PRA. Nonetheless, its passive (8b) is not possible. Then, what makes sentence (8b) an impossible passive? This is not accidental. We must reconsider (8a). The object seems to be a patient at first glance, but it is not; the object of (8a) has the semantic function of "comitative". Recollect that PRA requires that the object be a patient. Since sentence (8a) does not satisfy PRA, its passive (8b) is not possible. In (9a), the subject is not an agent. The sentence just describes a state, but not an action. Hence, its passive (9b) is not possible.

The verbs *marry* and *fit* may just describe some states. They can also describe some actions:

(10) a. Somebody (most probably, a priest) married John to Susan.
b. John was married to Susan (by a priest).

(11) a. The tailor fitted me.
b. I was fitted by the tailor.

Sentence (10b) is a possible passive, in contrast to the impossible passive (8b). This is not accidental, because the subject of its active sentence (10a) is an agent and its object is a patient. Sentence (11b) is also a possible passive, in contrast to the impossible passive sentence (9b). The subject of its active sentence (11a) is an agent. Here, an important question is: what is the full form of the following passive?

(12) John was married.

If we regard (8b) as the full form of the contracted passive (12), we are burdened with explaining why the full form is ungrammatical while its contracted form is grammatical. In contrast, if we regard (10b) as its full form, no such burden is required.

Now consider the following:

(13) a. Bill strikes/impresses Harry as pompous.
b. *Harry is struck/impressed by Bill as pompous.

In the active sentence (13a), the subject is not an agent: the object is not a patient, but an experiencer. Hence, the passive (13b) is not possible.

The verbs dealt with so far are what I call "middle" verbs. It is generally known that middle constructions cannot be passivized. Most literature regard this restriction just as a syntactic one. As shown above, however, this restriction is a semantic one, PRA, which is validated through middle constructions.

Peculiar Passives

Davison (1980) made a breakthrough for a special type of passives, what she calls "peculiar" passives. One characteristic of peculiar passives is that the object of the source active sentence is a prepositional object. It was traditionally known that only direct or indirect objects may be promoted to subjects through passivization. However, this is not necessarily true:

(14) a. Jack has sat on this chair.
b. This chair has been sat on by Jack.

(15) a. The famous boxer has slept in that bed.
b. That bed has been slept in by the famous boxer.

(16) a. The champion has driven to Chicago in an hour.
b. Chicago has been driven to by the champion in an hour.

As shown in the (b) sentences, prepositional objects may also be subjects of passive sentences. In this sense, Davison refers to such passives as "peculiar" passives. She indicates that sentence (14b), for example, suggests that the chair has suffered some damage as a result of Jack's sitting on it. This is a serious indication, suggesting that the subject of the active sentence (14a) is an agent, which caused some affection (= influence) on the object, which becomes a patient. Hence, the active (14a) satisfies PRA, which results in a possible passive (14b). The same thing can be said of (15) and (16). In the active (16a), the subject is an agent, and the prepositional object Chicago is somehow affected by the subject's driving to in an hour. Hence, PRA is satisfied, and the passive (16b) is possible. Thus, prepositional objects of locations in general may be promoted to subjects of the passives.

Now consider the following, in which the prepositional object is an instrument:

(17) a. Mary has cut potatoes with that knife too often without being sharpened.
b. That knife has been cut with too often without being sharpened.

In the active (17a), the subject is an agent, and the prepositional object is affected/influenced by the subject's action. Hence, the passive (17b) is possible under PRA.

Davison indicates that time, in general, does not permit passives:

(18) a. John and Sue quarrelled {before, during, after} dinner.
b. *Dinner was quarrelled {before, during, after} by John and Sue.

(19) a. Susan typed through the night.
b. *The night was typed through by Susan.

In the active (18a), the subjects are agents, but the prepositional object is not affected by their action. In the active (19a), the subject is an agent, but the prepositional object is not affected by the subject's action. Hence, the passives (18b) and (19b) are not possible under PRA. Davison notes that there are cases in which time expressions allow passives:

(20) a. All sat through dinner in stony silence.
b. Dinner was sat through by all in stony silence.

(21) a. We must live {through, during, before, after} this {hour, crisis, war}.
b. This {hour, crisis, war} must be lived {through, *during, *before, *after} by us.

These examples are quite interesting. The subjects in the passive sentences are not just time but rather events. Furthermore, the only possible preposition here is *through*, which implies some action involved. In the active (20a), *sit through* means *endure*, and in the active (21a), *live through* means *survive*. The subjects in the active sentences are agents, and the prepositional objects are patients. Thus, the possible passive sentences (20b) and (21b) are not accidental under PRA.

To sum up, Davison's study shows that locatives, instrumentals, and accompaniments are passivizable, whereas time, cause, manner and purpose are not passivizable. This dichotomy is related to the concrete and abstract axis.

I don't claim that the affection hypothesis (= PRA) accounts for all passives; what I claim is that my affection hypothesis works as far as middle constructions and "peculiar" passives are concerned. Davison's peculiarity is no more peculiar under PRA, or the affection hypothesis (cf. Yang 1999a).

Activo-passives

What Jespersen (1927) calls "activo-passive" means that the form has the active form, but its meaning is passive:

(22) a. The book sold quickly.
b. The cloth washes well.
c. The furniture polishes easily.
d. This shirt irons well.
e. His plays act well.
f. Food spoils quickly in summer.
g. Oysters make a good meal.
h. Beer and chocolate don't mix well.
i. This car drives easily.
j. The horse rides smoothly.
k. Bean curd digests easily.
l. Sheila seduces easily and willingly.
m. This scotch drinks easily.
n. His thesis reads easily.
o. Good tents put up in two minutes.

These sentences describe specific natures of the subjects. As seen in these sentences, some adverb is required to accompany the verb explicitly or implicitly. (22o) is an example of the implicit adverb (*in two minutes* = *quickly*).

Another characteristic of activo-passives is the primary responsibility anchored on the activity (cf. van Oosten 1977):

(23) a. John drives the car well.
b. The car drives well.

(23a) emphasizes John's good skill of driving, whereas (23b) emphasizes the car's good condition. The primary responsibility for the car's driving well is on the car itself, and possibly the secondary responsibility is on the driver, which is not important in (23b). However, this straightforward description is not necessarily adequate:

(24) a. John drives the car very well on this road.
b. The car drives very well on this road.
c. This road lets John drive the car very well.
d. This road lets the car drive very well.

My responsibility judgment is as follows. In (24a), the primary responsibility is on *this road*, the secondary is on *John*, and possibly the tertiary is on *the car*. In (24b), the primary is on *this road*, the secondary is on *the car*. In (24c), the primary is on *this road*, the secondary is on *John*, and the tertiary is on *the car*. In (24d), the primary is on *this road*, and the secondary is on *the car*. Out of the above sentences, (24b) is an activo-passive, which shows that the primary responsibility is not necessarily on the subject of an activo-passive, contra van Oosten (1977). That is, the primary responsibility may depend on the context.

Keyser & Roeper (1984) point out that activo-passives have non-eventive character; they generally cannot appear in imperative or progressive constructions:

(25) a. *Bribe easily, bureaucrats!
b. *Bureaucrats are bribing easily.

These data show that activo-passives express statives, but not eventives. Keyser & Roeper further indicate that activo-passives can occur in the progressive in appropriate contexts, just as statives can occur in the progressive in appropriate contexts:

(26) a. This book is reading better every day.
b. Bureaucrats are bribing more than ever in that president's second term.

(27) a. Young kids are knowing more and more about violence these days.
b. The baby is resembling his father more and more every day.

According to Keyser & Roeper (1984:38), activo-passives are generic statements, and therefore do not describe particular events in time:

(28) a. ?Yesterday, the mayor bribed easily according to the press.
b. ?At yesterday's house party, the kitchen wall painted easily.

These sentences are not fully grammatical, because they are particular time-bound, which does not accord with generic expressions. However, the fact that these sentences are marginal suggests that appropriate contexts may save activo-passives even in time-bound expressions:

(29) a. Chomsky's linguistics books sold well in 1960s.
b. (?)Yang's humor book did not sell well in 1998, the first year of publication.

These sentences are also time-bound, but they are felicitous in the contexts where the time expressions are sufficient to accomodate generic statements. It is not accidental that sentence (29a) is more grammatical than sentence (29b). This slight difference is due to the difference of time length, 1960s vs. 1998.

According to Keyser & Roeper (1984), activo-passives in the following are not grammatical, because their derived subjects (= underlying objects) are not affected:

(30) a. *French acquires easily.
b. *The arguments assume easily.
c. *The answer knows easily.

Incidentally, here the notion of "affectedness" accords with my "affection hypothesis" (= PRA) dealt with in the first part of this unit. Concerning the examples in (30), their underlying objects refer to the objects of the following:

(31) a. They acquire French easily.
b. They assume the arguments easily.
c. They know the answer easily.

I would like to raise a question about their grammatical judgments. It is hard to say that the object of (31a) is not affected. If my judgment is correct, the activo-passive (30a) is supposed to be grammatical, contra Keyser & Roeper (1984). I think the grammaticality of (30a) parallels the grammaticality of the following activo-passive (32b):

(32) a. They learn French easily.
b. French learns easily.

If native speakers of English accept (32b), while not accepting (30a), some explanation is required to the effect that verbs *learn* and *acquire* are different with respect to affection.

Un-passives

There are cases in which passives have no active sources:

(33) a. John was {rumored, alleged} to beat students.
b. *They {rumored, alleged} John to beat students.

It is known that the verbs *rumor* and *allege* have passive forms, but not active forms. The typical systematic case of this asymmetry is *un*-passives (cf. Siegel 1973):

(34) a. The president's blunder was unreported (in the press).
b. The brass knuckle was unpaid for.
c. Antarctica is uninhabited (by man).
d. The garbage went uncollected for a week.

In these examples, the underlined past participles are preceded by the negative prefix *un-*, which is the reason for the term "*un*-passive". The most striking feature of *un*-passives is the nonexistence of well-formed active sentences from which they could have been derived. The sentences in (34) have no active sources:

(35) a. *The press unreported the president's blunder.
b. *Someone unpaid for the brass knuckle.
c. *Man uninhabits Antarctica.
d. *Someone (went) uncollected the garbage for a week.

The ungrammaticality of these sentences is simply due to the fact that the underlined negative "*un*-verbs" do not exist.

In English, the negative prefix *un-* can be affixed only to adjectives and their adverb and noun forms, but not to verbs. The negativity of verbs is expressed by the syntactic device, but not by the morphological form:

(36) a. Don't do that. vs. *Undo that.
b. Don't zip the jacket. vs. *Unzip the jacket.

At this point, I must digress a little. Note that *undo* and *unzip* are possible verbs only for the sense of "reversative", which means "to get back to the original state". Consider the following:

(37) a. John is uncrowned.
b. The problem is unsolved.

These sentences have the same structure, but the former is ambiguous while the latter is not. (37a) means either (i) John is not (yet) crowned, or (ii) John is no more the king. That is, the one is the negative reading and the other is the reversative reading. (37b) has only the negative reading, but not the reversative reading. Then an interesting question is: what makes this difference? The answer is a pragmatic one. Pragmatically speaking, there are two categories: (i) things done can be undone, and (ii) things done cannot be undone. The first category includes verb pairs such as *button/unbutton, cap/uncap, crown/uncrown, do/undo, load/unload, say/unsay, zip/unzip*. The second category includes verbs such as *solve/ *unsolve, explain/*unexplain, kick/*unkick, kiss/*unkiss, know/unknow, remember/*unremember*. The second category means that something which has been done cannot be cancelled. We cannot find the starred verbs in the dictionary, simply because the real world does not allow such cancellations. However, we can find, in the dictionary, their past participles such as *unsolved, unexplained, unknown*, and *unremembered*, whose meanings are not the reversed states but the negated states. Such "*un*-V-*ed*" items are categorized as adjectives in the dictionary. This ends my digression.

Now returning to the main topic of *un*-passives, I will focus on the negative use of *un*-. The most serious concern is whether the negative prefix can be derived from the ordinary syntactic negation – let us call it NEG. There are myriads of reasons for rejecting that *un*- is a surface realization of NEG (Siegel 1973:304). In the first place, NEG creates ambiguities which do not arise with the morphological negative *un*-:

(38) a. Tom is not well because of the weather.
b. Tom is unwell because of the weather.

Sentence (38a) is ambiguous: (i) Tom is sick because of the weather, and (ii) Tom is well, not because of the weather but for some other reason. Sentence (38b), in contrast, is not ambiguous. It means only: Tom is sick because of the weather. Thus, NEG and *un*- differ with respect to the ability to create ambiguity. For further differences, see Siegel (1973). Technically speaking, NEG is a scope-bearing element, while *un*- is not (for scope ambiguity, see Yang 1993e).

Thus, the syntactic negation, NEG, cannot be the source for the *un*-passives. Then, the burden is on the lexical account:

(39) a. Verb's past participle → Adjective
b. Neg + adjective → *un*-Adjective
c. Lexical items in the dictionary: *unreported, unpaid uncollected, uninhabited*, etc.

On the basis of this lexical account, we can say that the past participles of *un*-passives are the "negative adjectives". The analysis in (39) can satisfy the syntactic aspects of *un*-passives. What remains unsolved in the analysis in (39) is the semantic aspect that the meaning of the *un*-passive is identical to one of the meanings of the NEG passive. This partial synonymy can be solved through semantic analysis, (which is not in the scope of this book).

Exercises and problems

1. Why is it that middle verb sentences cannot be passivized?
2. What is the difference of the following sentences?
   a. Susan is married to John.
   b. Susan is married by John.
3. Why is it that the term "middle" is confusing?
4. Why is it that activo-passives require specific adverbs?
5. Specify the primary and secondary responsibilities of the following:
   a. John drives the car well on this recently repaved road.
   b. The car drives well on this recently repaved road.
6. Is it true that activo-passives are generic expressions?
7. On what condition can time prepositional objects be passivized?
8. How is the concrete-abstract axis related to the peculiar passives?
9. Do prepositions pied-pipe or strand when prepositional objects are promoted to subjects?
10. Do *un*-passives have active sources?
11. What is the difference between the sentential negative NEG and the morphological negative *un*-?
12. Specify the ambiguity of the "*un*-verb" form.
13. Explain the following data, with respect to prepositions:
    a. *Some secrets of the planet are known by us.
    b. Some secrets of the planet are known to us.
    (cf. It is obvious to us that syntax is not easy.)

14. Compare the underlined parts of the following sentences. Why is it that the *best seller* in (b) cannot be replaced or paraphrased by the *best sellee*?
    a. John is a best seller.
    b. This book is a best seller.
15. Is the (a) sentence acceptable? If not, why? How about (b)?
    a. John was a/the best seller and this book is a/the best seller, too.
    b. John was, and this book is, a/the best seller. (by RNR)
16. Comment on the following data:
    (1) a. The two students have the same book.
        b. The two students have the same books.
    (2) a. The two diskettes have the same file.
        b. The two diskettes have the same files.
17. Explain the following data:
    a. John translates well. (ambiguous)
       (i) object-deleted reading; (ii) activo-passive reading
    b. Shakespeare translates well. (not ambiguous)
18. Discuss whether the following are active sentences or passive sentences:
    a. John is tired.
    b. John is gone.

Unit 25

Subject-Verb Inversion

In statement sentences, the subject occupies the initial position. In some cases, however, the subject yields the initial position to other elements for some reasons. Among them are "subject-auxiliary inverted" constructions and "subject-verb inverted" constructions. The former rule, Subject-Aux Inversion, was dealt with in Unit 7. The latter rule, Subject-Verb Inversion, is the subject of this unit.

The following illustrate the rule:

(1) a. A fountain stands in the garden.
    b. In the garden stands a fountain.

(2) a. The outside world is over that fence.
    b. Over that fence is the outside world.

(3) a. Bill raced into the opera house.
    b. Into the opera house raced Bill.

(4) a. My check for $1,000 is enclosed.
    b. Enclosed is my check for $1,000.

(5) a. The new way of life is far more significant than all this.
    b. Far more significant than all this is the new way of life.

As seen in these examples, the post-verb material is preposed for some reason, and concomitantly the subject and the verb are inverted. The verb here refers not to the verb alone but to the entire verb, which contains the verb and the auxiliary:

(6) a. The seeds of future realities may lie in his dreams.
b. In his dreams may lie the seeds of future realities.
(*Horizons USA* 34:38)

A significant question is: what causes/motivates the preposing of the post-verb material, which is called "core predicate" in Yang (1993b)? Intuitively speaking, the subject-verb-inverted (b) versions sound more natural than the (a) versions. This feeling accords with Green's pragmatic motivation. My view is this: the inversion is caused by the natural stream of thought/feeling. For example:

(7) a. Concerning the conquest of cancer, various ideas have been suggested throughout the world. Many medical doctors have invested a lot of energy, money, and time in this field. Dr. Kim is among them.
b. Concerning the conquest of cancer, ... Among them is Dr. Kim.

Comparing these two versions, it seems to me that the (b) version sounds more natural, because the stream of thought is more natural in (7b). I think this is the cause/motivation of the preposing of the core predicate. Similarly, in the following examples, the (b) version is more natural in the given discourse:

(8) a. The phenomenon induced by rhetorical questions of the type which Sadock (1975) has called queclatives is parallel to the conjunction and revelli examples just discussed.
b. Parallel to the conjunction and revelli examples just discussed is the phenomenon induced by rhetorical questions of the type which Sadock (1975) has called queclatives.

Concerning the subject-verb inversion, Green (1980:587) says:

> [T]he crucial aspect of these constructions is not really the inversion, but the preposing of the predicate; given preposing of these predicate types, *inversion seems to be required by the rules of grammar.*

She does not specify the italicized portion. It seems to me that once the core-predicate is preposed, the natural connection between the verb and the preposed core predicate is to be adjacent. This is the motivation for the inversion.

Now I will specify the preposable core predicates. The normal object cannot be preposed, simply because such an inversion results in the exchange of the subject and the object. I (Yang 1993b:28) set up the following core predicate types which are preposable:

(9) a. Adjectival: adjective, present and past participle, PP of adjectival use, infinitive of adjectival use
Main verb: copula *be*
b. Locational
Main verb: verbs of existence
c. Directional:
Main verb: action verbs
d. Quote-object:
Main verb: quoting verbs

In the above, the first three types are exemplified. The last type is illustrated below:

(10) a. John said the newspaper is late again.
b. "The newspaper is late again," said John.
c. "The newspaper," said John, "is late again."

The common feature of core predicate types is intransitivity. This feature rules out normal objects from the preposable core predicate types.

Another concern is whether the Subject-Verb Inversion also takes place in embedded sentences. Emonds (1976:35) indicates that "when embedded, the grammaticality varies":

(11) a. *A love for clothes that just as surprising was also got her into debt.
b. ?Bill is happy that on the porch is a large wicker couch.
c. ?We convinced the authorities that more important would be the establishment of legal services.
d. We assume that among the extensional spatial-temporal relations are the three relations mentioned above.

I think that the difference of grammaticality of these sentences is the reflection of the degree of complexity (i.e. readability). Compare (11c) and (11d). Their main verbs are different with respect to the assertivity degree. The verb *convince* cannot be used as a parenthetical, whereas the verb *assume* can be (cf. Unit 22). I guess this assertivity difference is related with the degree of grammaticality of (11c) and (11d). My another guess is that many native speakers may accept (11b).

Still another concern on the Subject-Verb Inversion is the heaviness of the subject. Green (1980:586) refutes the "heavy subject" account, for the reason that the versions where the heavy subjects are not inverted are also "grammatical":

(12) a. Supporting merger were Lachlan Blair, Mary Blair, Phillips Garman, Linda Bronston, and David Linstrom. (Green's (8a))
b. Lachlan Blair, Mary Blair, . . . , and David Linstrom (all) were supporting merger. (Green's (9a))

(13) a. Dead were the pilot, Robert Conduff Jr., 38, Fort Hood, Texas,

Theresa's step-father, her mother, Francis Conduff, 48, and her half-sister, Maria Francis Foster, 14. (Green's (8b))

b. The pilot, Robert Conduff Jr., 38, Fort Hood, Texas, Theresa's step-father, her mother, Francis Conduff, 48, and her half-sister, Maria Francis Foster, 14 all died. (Green's (9b))

In the (b) versions, the subjects are very heavy. As Green mentions, these sentences are "grammatical". What is serious, however, is the degree of "acceptability". Which is more acceptable in each of (12) and (13)? The answer is very simple: in the situations like the above, which versions will the reporters choose?

Thus, I claim, contra Green, that the subject's "heaviness" is not irrelevant to the cause/motivation of the inversion. While reading books and articles, I noticed the following examples, in which the subjects are very heavy:

(14) a. Fairly common is the use of a verb that represents normal customary action of a thing to suggest that the thing is there. (Bolinger 1977:97)

b. Especially unoverthankable are the students and friends of the Department of Linguistics, whose words and labors sanctioned the materialization of both the Fifteenth Regional Meeting itself and the present volumes. (*CLS* 15:Preface)

c. Of further interest is the fact that in terms of recovery, the authors found no significant difference between the below 10 and above 10 age groups . . . (William Ritchie (ed.). 1978. *Second Language Acquisition*. p. 14)

d. At the heart of this long-term issue in Asia lies the need to develop stable political institutions to succeed present authoritative regimes. (*Time* 5/21/1979. p. 32)

I have a big collection of such examples. The above examples are good enough to justify that the subject's heaviness is relevant to the cause/motivation of the Subject-Verb Inversion. For further details of the rule, see Green (1980) and Yang (1993b).

Exercises and problems

1. What post-verb materials can be preposed in SVI?
2. Why is it that the normal object cannot be preposed?
3. What is/are the cause(s)/motivation(s) of the Subject-Verb Inversion?
4. Is Heavy NP Shift related to Subject-Verb Inversion?
5. Is there any relation between the fact that adjectives cannot be freely placed in the cleft focus position (cf. Unit 9) and the fact that adjective preposing triggers SVI?
6. Is there any relation between SVI-sentences and WH-question sentences?

Unit 26

Sluicing

This rule is one of deletion rules. This rule deletes everything but the preposed constituent of an embedded question, under the condition that the remainder of the question is identical to some other part of the sentence, or of a preceding sentence (cf. Ross 1969:252). The following illustrate the rule:

(1) a. Somebody just left. Guess who just left.
b. Somebody just left. Guess who.

(2) a. John is going to invite somebody from Seoul to the party, but they don't know who he's going to invite to the party.
b. . . . , but they don't know who.

(3) a. Bill is writing something, but I can't imagine

[what / where / why / how / how fast / to whom / with whom / for whom] he is writing.

b. Bill is writing something,

but I can't imagine [what / where / why / how / how fast / to whom / with whom / for whom]

As seen above, everything except the question word can be deleted in the second sentence/conjunct. This deletion is possible because the deleted part can easily be recovered from the first sentence/conjunct.

The non-sluiced and sluiced versions can undergo Extraposition:

(4) a. I know that Sue is studying, but what she is studying isn't clear.
b. I know that Sue is studying, but it isn't clear what she is studying.
c. I know that Sue is studying, but what isn't clear.
d. I know that Sue is studying, but it isn't clear what.

Sentence (4b) is derived from sentence (4a) by Extra. Sentence (4c) is derived from sentence (4a) by Sluicing. Sentence (4d) is derived from sentence (4c) by Extra.

One recalcitrant problem is prepositions. Prepositions are supposed to be pied-piped with their nominals. Nonetheless, they may be stranded:

(5) a. Susan was dancing, but I don't know with whom she was dancing.
b. Susan was dancing, but I don't know <u>with whom.</u>
c. Susan was dancing, but I don't know whom she was dancing with.
d. Susan was dancing, but I don't know <u>whom with.</u>

The contrast of (5b) and (5d) is the reflection of the contrast of (5a) and

(5c). This shows that *with* may be pied-piped or stranded in the context. In contrast, *under* does not strand in the following examples:

(6) a. He would report me under some circumstances, but I can only guess under which circumstances he would report me.
b. He would report me under some circumstances, but I can only guess under which.
c. *He would report me under some circumstances, but I can only guess which circumstances he would report me under.
d. *He would report me under some circumstances, but I can only guess which under.

The contrast of (6b) and (6d) is the reflection of the contrast of (6a) and (6c). The ungrammaticality of (6c) seems to be related with the "linkability" between *which circumstances* and *under*, although I cannot specify the exact condition. The linkability is also reflected in the following sentences:

(7) a. Under what circumstances will the earth implode?
b. *What circumstances will the earth implode under?

Concerning preposition stranding, the linguistics literature are very silent. I have consulted many eminent English linguists about preposition stranding. But no clear answer is yet available (cf. Unit 13).

In the following, question words occur more than once:

(8) a. We are going somewhere today. Who knows where we are going today?
b. We are going somewhere today. Who knows where?

(9) a. We will do something somewhere somehow someday for some purpose.
b. Who knows what, where, how, when, and why?

The acceptability of (9b) requires appropriate contexts.

The question word *whether* is exceptional:

(10) a. Bob can't decide whether to quit smoking or not, and Bill can't decide whether to, either.

b. *Bob can't decide whether to quit smoking or not, and Bill can't decide whether, either.

The difference of the grammatical sentence (10a) and the ungrammatical sentence (10b) is relevant to the fact that two different rules are applied. In (10a), VP Deletion (to be dealt with in Unit 28) is applied, and in (10b), Sluicing is applied.

The more interesting exception is the question word *why*:

(11) a. John knows why he has to study hard, but Mary doesn't know why.

b. *John knows why he has to study hard, but Mary doesn't know why to.

In the grammatical sentence (11a), Sluicing is applied. In the ungrammatical sentence (11b), VP Deletion is applied. Such an exceptional behavior of *why* is restricted not only to VP Deletion. The sequence of *why to* is allowed under no conditions:

(12) a. We wonder {what, when. where, how, whether, *why} to eat.

b. what to do, who/whom to help, when to start, where to go, how to survive, whether to marry vs. *why to live

Interesting is the fact that *why* also behaves differently from other WH-words, with respect to WH-*ever* formation:

(13) whatever, whoever, whenever, wherever, however vs. *whetherever, *whyever

In the case of **whetherever*, its absence is due to the semantic mismatch. In the case of **whyever*, in contrast, its absence is not due to the semantic mismatch. Then, the curious question is: why is it that *why* behaves differently from other WH-words? I have consulted many eminent English linguists about the absence of *why to* and *whyever*, but no answer is available. I will present my explanation. The matter hinges on the difference of "any target" vs. the "specific target" of a sentence. *Why* can have its target on any element of a sentence, while the other Wh-words have their targets on specific elements of a sentence. This difference can be rephrased by the difference of any non-specific target of *why* vs. some specific targets of other Wh-words. Infinitives connote some specific actions/states. Some specific action/state is not compatible with *why*, which is relevant to any non-specific target. On the other hand, some specific action/state of an infinitive is compatible with other Wh-words, which are relevant to specific targets (cf. Yang 1999d).

Also, interesting is the fact that *why* and *whether* behave differently from other WH-words, with respect to WH-*ever* formation:

(14) a. whatever, whoever, whenever, wherever, however
b. *whyever, *whetherever

In the case of *whether*, it has already incorporated the sense of *-ever*. Hence, *whetherever* is self-contradictory as well as redundant. In the case of *why*, the correct reason (i.e. whyness) requires some unique reason, but not any reason. Hence, *why* is not compatible with *-ever* (cf. Yang 1999d).

Exercises and problems

1. How much can be sluiced?
2. What is the function of Sluicing?
3. Why is it that *whether* is exceptional in the formation of WH-*ever*?
4. Why is it that **why to* and **whyever* are not possible?
5. What are sources of *For what*? and *What for*? Is there any meaning or use difference between the two question forms?
6. Is Sluicing involved in the following?

   (1) a. I know that John is not a swindler.
       b. I know not.

   (2) a. I like my humor book, although nobody wants to buy it.
       b. I like my humor book, though.

   (3) a. I want to take a shower.
       b. Me, too.

   (4) a. (It's) ten minutes after 8 o'clock/the hour.
       b. (It's) ten minutes after.

   (5) a. What will happen if the young students fall in love?
       b. What if the young students fall in love?

Unit 27

Gapping

If the verbs of two (or more) clauses in a sentence are the same, the verb in the second clause/conjunct may be deleted, which results in a gap in the sentence. Hence, the rule is called "Gapping". The following illustrate the rule:

(1) a. Sam studies linguistics and Bill studies philosophy.
    b. Sam studies linguistics and Bill [e] philosophy.

(2) a. Kurt plays the krumhorn, Ivan plays the alphorn, Frank plays the fluegelhorn, and Boris plays the bassethorn.
    b. Kurt plays the krumhorn, Ivan [e] the alphorn, Frank [e] the fluegelhorn, and Boris [e] the bassethorn.

(3) a. I want to try to begin to write a novel, and John wants to try to begin to write a play.
    b. I want to try to begin to write a novel,
    and John [e] to try to begin to write a play.
    [e] to begin to write a play.
    [e] to write a play.
    [e] a play.

As in (3a), if the same verb is more than one, the gappable sentence is more than one, as shown in (3b).

In the case of embedding, Gapping applies only if the complementizer is absent from the second clause (cf. Jackendoff 1977:45):

(4) a. It is hard to believe that Jack hates swimming and that Fred hates surfing.
b. *It is hard to believe that Jack hates swimming and that Fred [e] surfing.
c. It is hard to believe that Jack hates swimming and [e] Fred [e] surfing.

(5) a. For Jack to hate swimming and for Fred to hate surfing would be a tremendous surprise.
b. *For Jack to hate swimming and for Fred [e] surfing would be a tremendous surprise.
c. For Jack to hate swimming and [e] Fred [e] surfing would be a tremendous surprise.

The ungrammaticality of the (b) versions is due to the presence of the complementizers *that* and *for* in the second conjuncts.

The cause/motivation of any deletion is to economize the expression, especially the repeated part. Despite such a good motivation, reduced sentences may cause uninvited ambiguity. On this matter, Hankamer (1973) claims: "any application of Gapping which would yield an output structure identical to a structure by Gapping from another source, but with the "gap" at the left extremity, is disallowed." This condition is referred to as the no-ambiguity condition (for short, NAC).

According to Hankamer's judgment, the (a) sentences refer to the (b) sentences, not the (c) sentences in the following:

(6) a. Jack calls Joe Mike and Sam Harry. (gapped sentence)
b. Jack calls Joe Mike and [Jack calls] Sam Harry.
c. Jack calls Joe Mike and Sam [calls Joe] Harry.

(7) a. Jack told Harry that Nixon was a fairy, and Alex that Agnew had warts. (gapped sentence)

b. Jack told Harry that Nixon was a fairy, and [Jack told] Alex that Agnew had warts.
c. Jack told Harry that Nixon was a fairy, and Alex [told Harry] that Agnew had warts.

(8) a. Max wanted to put the eggplant on the table, and Harvey in the sink. (gapped sentence)
b. Max wanted to put the eggplant on the table, and [Max wanted to put] Harvey in the sink.
c. Max wanted to put the eggplant on the table, and Harvey [wanted to put the eggplant] in the sink.

(9) a. The press characterized Agnew as colorless, and Nixon as low-keyed. (gapped sentence)
b. The press characterized Agnew as colorless, and [the press characterized] Nixon as low-keyed.
c. The press characterized Agnew as colorless, and Nixon [characterized Agnew] as low-keyed.

The brackets in the (b) and (c) sentences mean that those parts are deleted in the (a) sentences. Hankamer's intention is this: the (a) sentences are derived from the (b) sentences by Gapping, and they cannot be derived from the (c) sentences. This interpretation accords with his NAC. I am not a native speaker of English, but my own interpretation accords with Hankamer's, except for (8).

However, Channon (1975) objects to Hankamer's claim. Channon's criticism of Hankamer goes as follows: (i) NAC is not a universal condition (cf. Russian) and (ii) its validity even for English is not uncontroversial. He indicates that the intent of NAC is to restrict Gapping in such a way that the deletion cite must be as far to the left as structurally possible.

Channon further indicates three difficulties with Hankamer's view.

The first difficulty: there are gradations of acceptability among sentences which NAC rules out in an undifferentiated way. According to NAC, the (b) readings (= left-peripheral gaps) are possible, while the (c) readings (= internal gaps) should be equally (= with no difference of degree) unacceptable. However, the informant test shows that acceptability is subject to idiolectal variation. (I do not cite Channon's concrete examples.)

The second problem: the acceptability of certain gapped sentences which are ruled out by NAC seems to vary with the heaviness of what is left behind, at least for some speakers:

(10) a. ??Tom reads the newspaper quickly, and Sandra carefully.
b. ?Tom reads the newspaper over breakfast, and Sandra over lunch.
c. Tom reads the newspaper in the morning, and Sandra in the afternoon.
d. Tom reads the newspaper on the way to work, and Sandra after she gets there.
e. Tom reads the newspaper in the morning on the way to work, and Sandra over coffee after she gets there.

The third difficulty: there are three types of counterexamples.

(11) a. Massachusetts elected McCormack Congressman, and Pennsylvania, Schweiker.

(12) a. Max writes plays in the bedroom, and Harvey in the basement.

(13) a. Schachter has informed me that the basic order in Tagalog and related languages is VOS; Goddard that the unmarked order in Algonkian is OVS; and Carden that the best order in Aleut is OSV.

Although I am not a native speaker of English, my own interpretations of these sentences are not the (b) versions but the (c) versions:

(11) b. *. . . , and [Massachusetts elected] Pennsylvania Schweiker.
c. . . . , and Pennsylvania [elected] Schweiker [Congressman].

(12) b *. . . , and [Max writes] Harvey in the basement.
c. . . . , and Harvey [writes plays] in the basement.

(13) b. *. . . ; and [Schachter has informed] Goddard that the unmarked order in Algonkian is OVS; . . .
c. . . . ; and Goddard [has informed me] that the unmarked order in Algonkian is OVS; . . .

It should be seriously noted that my intuitive interpretations are: in the case of Hankamer's examples (6–9), I choose the (b) versions (= left-peripheral gap readings); in the case of Shannon's examples (11–13), by contrast, I choose the (c) versions (= internal gap readings). This difference definitely suggests that the acceptability of gapped sentences depends on the semantic and/or pragmatic information of the gapped sentences.

Kuno (1976) advocates a functional approach. He contends that Hankamer's data fall out from his functional constraints. For details, see Kuno (1976), which deserves our attention.

Jake (1977) posits two criteria: (i) pragmatic parallelism, and (ii) factivity hierarchy. The criterion of pragmatic parallelism means: in assigning a reading to an ambiguous gapped conjunct, a hearer establishes a pragmatic parallel between the gapped conjunct and the ungapped conjunct, based on the hearer's assumption about what the speaker knows about a given context for a particular utterance and what is pragmatically plausible in the real world. For example:

(14) The press characterized Nixon as colorless and the networks as low-keyed.

In (14), the internal gap is the preferred reading, which is based on the relationship of the press and the networks.

(15) The press characterized Barbara Walters as colorless and the networks as low-keyed.

In (15), the left gap is the preferred reading. It is the pragmatic relationship of the individual to the networks which causes the left gap to be preferred.

(16) Bob persuaded me to pick up the sandwiches and Tom the liquor.

Sentence (16) is ambiguous, depending on the context. Suppose that both Tom and I are less cooperative for preparing the party. In this context, the left gap reading is preferred. Suppose next that both Bob and Tom are cooperative and only I am less cooperative. In this context, the internal gap reading is preferred. Thus, Jake's pragmatic parallelism is intuitively appealing.

At this point, it is relevant to cite Lakoff's (1973:442) classic "scratch" sentences:

(17) a. John scratched his leg and so did Bill.
b. John scratched his leg and so did Mary.

The ambiguity here is concerned with "whose leg Bill and Mary scratched". It depends on the relation between the subjects of the two conjuncts, and furthermore on the cultural difference. These examples support Jake's pragmatic parallelism.

As shown thus far, the interpretations of gapped sentences definitely require pragmatic factors. For Jake's factivity hierarchy, see his paper.

Exercises and problems

1. What is the motivation for Gapping?
2. In English, Gapping operates only in the second conjunct. Why not in the first conjunct? What about in your mother tongue?
3. How much can be gapped?
4. Why is it that there may be discrepancy between the speaker's gapping and the hearer's interpretation of it?
5. What rule is involved in each of the following?

    a. A: I would like to order t-bone steak.
       B: Me too.

    b. A: You shouldn't touch such meat.
       B: Why not?
6. Is there any similarity between Gapping and Parasitic Gap? (cf. Engdahl 1983, Sag 1983)

Unit 28

VP Deletion, *Do-So* Rule and *So*-Aux Rule

VP Deletion

The following illustrate VP Deletion:

(1) a. Joan adopted a child because she wanted to adopt a child.
b. *Joan adopted a child because she wanted.
c. Joan adopted a child because she wanted to.

(2) a. Can you tell me what the Korean peninsula looks like?
b. *Yes, I'm glad.
c. Yes, I'm glad to.

One might wonder why the (b) versions are not grammatical. If the (b) versions are also grammatical, two rules are involved: Infinitive Complement Deletion, which yields the (b) versions, and VP Deletion, which yields the (c) versions. However, what is involved here is VP Deletion: Infinitive Complement Deletion does not exist. Hence, only the (c) versions are grammatical. VP consists of [verb-stem + (object)], which excludes the infinitive complementizer *to*. For VP, see Unit 10.

Consider the following:

(3) a. I heard that Tom went to Paris, but I don't know why he went to

Paris.

b. . . . , but I don't know why he did. (VP Deletion)

c. . . . , but I don't know why. (Sluicing)

(4) Mike [built a house / is building a house / may build a house / must have been building a house / has a house / is tired]

and John [did / is / may / must have been / has/does / is] too.

In (3b), the auxiliary *did* ends the sentence. This is not accidental, because *went to Paris* means *did go to Paris*, in which the auxiliary constituent and the VP constituent are clearly distinguished (cf. Unit 10). The examples in (4) clearly show the distinction between Aux constituent and VP constituent.

Now consider the following from Kuno (1975):

(5) A: Did John hit Mary with a stick or with a belt?

B: a. He hit her with a belt.

b. *He did [e] with a belt.

(6) A: Where was John robbed?

B: a. He was robbed in Paris.

b. *He was [e] in Paris.

(7) A: Why did John hit Mary?
B: a. He hit her because he hated her.
b. *He did [e] because he hated her.

(8) A: With whom did John want to go to Paris?
B: a. He wanted to go there with Mary.
b. *He wanted to [e] with Mary.

(9) A: How does John want to go to Paris?
B: a. He wants to go there by boat.
b. *He wants to [e] by boat.

In these examples, the (b) versions are all ungrammatical. In order to account for this fact, one might hypothesize: "VP Deletion can apply only at the sentence-final position." This hypothesis would account for (5–9) and the following as well:

(10) A: Will John do this?
B: Yes, he will [e], willingly.

(11) A: Was John robbed?
B: Yes, he was [e], in Paris.

(12) A: Did John hit Mary?
B: Yes, he did [e], because he hated her.

The (B) versions are grammatical only on the assumption that there is a pause before the adverbial, which is given as after-thought.

However, the above hypothesis cannot account for the following:

(13) A: Why did John want to go to Paris?
B: He wanted to [e] because Mary was there.

(14) Mary was not robbed in Paris, but she was [e] in London.

(15) Mary did not visit museums in Paris, but she did [e] in London.

These sentences do not require the pause that sentences (10–12) do, and therefore, it is not easy to claim that the adverbial elements after the deletion sites are outside *he wanted to* in (13B), *she was* in (14), and *she did* in (15).

Thus, Kuno posits the following constraint:

(16) The Constraint on VP Deletion
VP Deletion can apply only to the VP that is VP-final.

For the understanding of Kuno's constraint, we need to invoke some formal technicality which involves tree diagrams. However, I would not like to enter into such a technicality. I, instead, will show the constraint informally. Kuno's constraint requires us to distinguish between (i) the VP that is VP-final (= the VP-final VP), and (ii) the VP that is not VP-final (= the VP-nonfinal VP):

(17) a. Did he hit her?
b. Yes, he hit her.
c. Yes, he did [e].

(18) a. Why did he want to go to Paris?
b. He wanted to go there because Mary was there.
c. He wanted to [e] because Mary was there.

(19) a. Did he hit her with a belt?
b. Yes, he hit her with a belt.
c. *Yes, he did [e] with a belt.

(20) a. Why did he hit her?
b. He hit her because he hated her.
c. *He did [e] because he hated her.

According to Kuno's constraint, the underlined part of (17b) is a VP-final VP. Therefore, it can be deleted, as in (17c). The underlined part of (18b) is also a VP-final VP because *go there* and *because Mary was there* are not in a single constituent. Therefore, the underlined part can be deleted, as in (18c). The underlined part of (19b) is not a VP-final VP, because *hit her* and *with a belt* are in a single constituent. Therefore, the underlined part cannot be deleted, as shown in (19c). The underlined part of (20b) is not a VP-final VP, because *hit her* and *because he hated her* are in a single constituent.

Our curiosity about the above explanation is the contrast of the *because*-clause of (18) and the *because*-clause of (20). According to Kuno, the contrast hinges on whether a VP and the rest are in a single constituent or not. This specification is very confusing because any adjacent elements may be in a single constituent at some high(er) node in a tree.

For this reason, I suggest that the contrast under consideration must be understood this way: in (18), *go there* and *because Mary was there* are cognitively not so closely linked. In (20), by contrast, *hit her* and *because he hated her* are cognitively so closely linked. That is, a VP cannot be deleted if it has a closely linked mate, because this VP is not a VP-final VP. For further details, see Kuno (1975).

Do-So Rule and *So*-Aux Rule

The following illustrate the rules:

(21) a. John burned Yang's humor book, and Bill burned Yang's humor book, too.
b. John burned Yang's humor book, and Bill did so, too.
c. John burned Yang's humor book, and so did Bill.

If the strings of "verb and the rest" of the two conjuncts are the same, that of the second conjunct may be replaced by *do so*. This rule is called *Do-So* Rule, which changes (21a) to (21b). Or that of the second conjunct may be replaced by "*so* aux". This rule is called *So*-Aux Rule, which changes (21a) to (21c). The formal difference of the two rules is this: the former is followed by *too*, while the latter lacks it.

The following show the difference with respect to constraints:

(22) a. John knows the answer, and Bill knows the answer, too.
b. *John knows the answer, and Bill does so, too.
c. John knows the answer, and so does Bill.

(23) a. John is heavy, and Bill is heavy, too.
b. *John is heavy, and Bill does so, too.
c. John is heavy and so is Bill.

(24) a. John is careful, and Bill is careful, too.
b. *John is careful, and Bill does so, too.
c. John is careful, and so is Bill.

The (b) versions are not grammatical, which means that *Do-So* Rule does not apply if the predicate is a stative verb or an adjective. This means that the *do* of *Do-So* Rule is the "pro-verb" of action or activity. In contrast, *So*-Aux Rule is not subject to such constraints, because the rule does not contain *do*, which is the pro-verb of action or activity. *Do* in the *So*-Aux Rule is the auxiliary *do* (e.g. *So can/will/do I*).

Lakoff and Ross (1976) use *Do-So* Rule for the test of VP constituency. They claim that "*do-so*" replaces all of the constituents of VP and only these. Thus, elements that may occur after *do-so* are outside VP (i.e. are not constituents of VP), and elements that cannot so occur are inside VP. This test shows that DOs, IOs of *to*-NP, directional adverbs, and some place adverbs are inside VP:

(25) a. John cut the cake, and Mary did so, too. (DO)
b. *John cut the cake, and Mary did so the tape.

(26) a. John gave a gift to Sue, and Bill did so, too. (IO of *to*-NP)
b. *John gave a gift to Sue, and Bill did so to Mary.

(27) a. John loaded furniture onto the truck, and Bill did so, too. (directional adv)
b. *John loaded furniture onto the truck, and Bill did so onto the wagon.

(28) a. I remained in England, and John did so, too. (place adv)
b. *I remained in England, and John did so in France.

(29) a. I solved the problem in England, and John did so, too.
b. I solved the problem in England, and John did so in France.

In (25–27), the (b) versions are not grammatical, which shows that DO, IO of *to*-NP, and directional adverb are inside VP. The reason is this: the category already covered by *do-so* is not compatible with another example of the same category. For example, (25b) means *John cut the cake, and*

Mary cut the cake (= Mary did so) the tape, which is not grammatical. In (28) and (29), the same place adverb, *in England/France*, is involved. Here, (28b) is not grammatical, while (29b) is grammatical. This difference is the reflection of the contrast of the place adverb *in England/France*, It is inside VP in (28b) whereas it is outside VP in (29b), following the same rationale as that involved in (25–27).

This test shows that IOs of *for*-NP, time adverbs, *because*-clauses, and *if*-clauses are outside VP:

(30) a. Bill bought a car for Mary, and I'll do so for Susan, too. (IO of *for*-NP)
b. John took a trip last summer, and I'm going to do so this summer. (time adverb)
c. Smith voted for John because he thought John was good, but I did so because other candidates were evil. (*because*-clause)
d. John would take the job if they paid $5,000, but I would do so if they paid me $10,000. (*if*-clause)

These sentences are all grammatical, which means that the categories indicated above are outside VP: they are not constituents of VP. In this regard, the test of VP constituent by *Do-So* Rule is informative as well as interesting.

Exercises and problems

1. Why is it that the *to* which precedes VP is not deleted in the process of VP Deletion?
2. Explicate Kuno's Constraint on VP Deletion.

3. Is it possible to explain Kuno's data by the "linkability" account?
4. Compare VP Deletion and *Do-So* Rule.
5. Compare *Do-So* Rule and *So*-Aux Rule.
6. What is the difference between (a) and (b)?
    a. I don't think so.
    b. I think otherwise.
7. How do we know whether some element is inside or outside VP?

Unit 29

Minor Deletion Rules

In this unit, I deal with some minor deletion rules such as Object Deletion, *That* Deletion, and *To-Be* Deletion.

Object Deletion

Transitive verbs necessarily require objects. However, some transitive verbs can go without objects. Such verbs include: *cook, drink, dress/undress, eat, kiss, marry, read, wash.*

(1) a. I want to drink [e].
    b. I want to drink water/some soft drink.
    c. I want to drink alcoholic beverage.

Suppose that somebody utters (1a), which has no object. Sentence (1a) can be interpreted as (1b), but not as (1c). This shows that only unmarked objects can be omitted. This generalization, however, is subject to contextual constraints:

(2) a. Context: at a drinking party.
    b. I want to drink [e].
    c. I want to drink [e] too.

In the specific context (2a), sentence (2b) may mean either (1b) or (1c). Sentence (2c) definitely means (1c) only.

Incidentally, Mittwoch (1982) claims that *eating* and *eating something* are different: the former is an activity while the latter is an accomplishment. For details, see Mittwoch (1982), and for the notions of activity and achievement, see Vendler (1967). Fillmore (1986:98–99) indicates that some of "closely synonymous verbs" permit Object Deletion, while others do not:

	(A) Omissible	(B) Non-omissible
(3)	She promised [e].	*She pledged/vowed/guaranteed [e].
(4)	I tried [e].	*I attempted [e].
(5)	They accepted [e].	*They endorsed [e].
(6)	They approved [e].	*They acknowledged [e].
(7)	She found out [e].	*She discovered [e].
(8)	I'm waiting [e].	*I'm awaiting [e].
(9)	When did you leave [e]?	*When did you vacate [e]?
(10)	I protest [e].	*I oppose [e].

This distinction is not accidental, I think. Object omissible cases involve "unmarked" verbs, while object non-omissible cases involve "marked" verbs.

Fillmore (1986:101–102) further indicates that, although verbs are unmrked, some objects are omissible while others are not:

	(A) Omissible	(B) Non-omissible
(11)	They accepted my offer.	They accepted my gift.
	They accepted [e].	*They accepted [e].
(12)	I applied for the job.	They applied the bandage.
	I applied [e].	*They applied [e].

(13)	They approached me. They approached [e].	They approached the solution. *They approached [e].
(14)	They closed the shop early. They closed [e] early.	She closed the drawer. *She closed [e].
(15)	They know that he resigned. They know [e].	They know Louisa. *They know [e].
(16)	She left home. She left [e].	She left this package. *She left [e].
(17)	We returned to the camp. We returned [e].	We returned to the task. *We returned [e].
(18)	I see that they're here. I see [e].	I see the rat. *I see [e].

Here again, the distinction is not accidental, I think. Object omissible cases involve unmarked elements, while object non-omissible cases involve marked elements. Any deletion or contraction is prohibited unless the missing element or part is recoverable. Recoverability is much easier in the case of unmarked members. In the case of marked members, recoverability requires specific contexts.

That Deletion

There are some contexts in which *that* can occur: (i) relative clauses, (ii) content clauses, and (iii) sentential complements. Since the case of relative clauses is well known, I will deal with the other two cases.

I will consider sentential complements first. Pope (1975) points out that the complementizer *that* can be deleted (i) if the main verb is non-factive, or (ii) if the subject is definite in case the verb is factive:

(19) a. I think that girl student smokers will outnumber boy student smokers.
b. I think [e] girl student smokers will outnumber boy student smokers.

(20) a. It's odd that the best student failed the final exam.
b. It's odd [e] the best student failed the final exam.

(21) a. It's odd that a diligent student cut the class.
b. *It's odd [e] a diligent student cut the class.

(22) a. I regret that young students smoke more and more.
b. *I regret [e] young students smoke more and more.

The *that*-less sentence (19b) is grammatical because the main verb is non-factive. *Odd* is a factive predicate. The contrast of (20b) and (21b) is that of the definiteness of the complement subject in (20b) and the indefiniteness of the complement subject in (21b). (22b) is not grammatical, because the main verb is factive and the complement subject is indefinite.

Pope's account hinges on factivity of the main verbs and it is intuitively appealing. In addition, he invokes the contrast of definite and indefinite complement subjects. This second feature is quite curious, which calls for explanation.

If the complementizer *that* is deletable in statements, it can also be deletable in WH-questions:

(23) a. You wish (that) you'd married somebody else.
b. Who do you wish (that) you'd married?

(24) a. You think (that) we should wait for some hours.
b. How long do you think (that) we should wait?

(25) a. You said (that) you wanted something for Christmas.
b. What did you say (that) you wanted for Christmas?

Rosenbaum (1967:39) indicates that the deletion of the complementizer *that* is prohibited if some material (except the object NP) intervenes the main predicate and the complementizer:

(26) a. I doubt that John came yesterday quite seriously.
b. I doubt [e] John came yesterday quite seriously.
c. I doubt quite seriously that John came yesterday.
d. *I doubt quite seriously [e] John came yesterday.

(27) a. It is important to John that you are here on time.
b. *It is important to John [e] you are here on time.

(28) a. I convinced Bill that John was not so bad.
b. *I convinced Bill [e] John was not so bad.

Now consider the following, where content clauses are involved:

(29) a. I have a notion that UN can pacify the hard-to-persuade country.
b. I have a notion [e] UN can pacify the hard-to-persuade country.

(30) a. I have an idea that the boy will marry the tall girl.
b. I have an idea [e] the boy will marry the tall girl.

Note that the sequence of *have a notion/idea* means *think*. Hence, the reason that the complementizer may be deleted is clear.

The account of the following data is not easy and simple:

(31) a. The rumor that the couple will divorce is unconfirmed.
b. The rumor [e] the couple will divorce is unconfirmed.

(32) a. The fact that Sam was a fool was feared by John.
b. The fact [e] Sam was a fool was feared by John.

(33) a. The fact that John was here surprised me.
b. *The fact [e] John was here surprised me.

The reason why (32b) is grammatical while (33b) is not is not known. I advise non-native speakers of English not to delete the complementizer *that* which is between head nouns and content clauses (cf. Brame 1979:99).

To-Be Deletion

This deletion depends on the main verb. If the main verb is a verb such as: *believe, consider, deem, find, imagine, regard, seem, think,* etc, *to-be* can be deleted :

(34) a. I think Bill (to be) a genius.
b. Bill is thought (to be) a genius.

(35) a. I imagine Bill (to be) happy.
b. Bill is imagined (to be) happy.

(36) a. I found Sue (to be) exhausted.
b. Sue was found (to be) exhausted.

(37) Bill appears (to be) intelligent.

(38) Everyone seems (to be) satisfied

If the main verb is a verb such as: *expect, happen, want,* etc., *to-be* cannot be deleted:

(39) a. I expect John to be smart.
b. *I expect John [e] smart.

(40) a. John happened to be satisfied.
b. *John happened [e] satisfied.

(41) a. I want John to be president.
b. *I want John [e] president.

It should be noted that if the main verb is a verb such as: *elect, feel, name, paint, make,* etc., *to-be* is not allowed:

(42) a. We elected Bill the director.
b. *We elected Bill to be the director.

(43) a. Everyone feels satisfied.
b. *Everyone feels to be satisfied.

(44) a. They named the first child "Tori".
b. *They named the first child to be "Tori".

(45) a. We painted the house blue.
b. *We painted the house to be blue.

Ross (1973) indicates that if the main verb is *want* or *would like*, *to-be* may be deleted, and that *to-be* cannot be deleted if its subject has been produced by a prior application of Raising-to-Object:

(46) a. I want a lazy man (to be) hungry.
b. I want the facts (to be) accurate.

(47) a. I want it to be certain that you will pass the exam.
b. I want it [e] certain that you will pass the exam.

(48) a. I want you to be certain to pass the exam.
b. *I want you [e] certain to pass the exam.

Concerning the data in (47) and (48), what Ross intends to indicate is this: *it* in (47a) is produced by Extra, whereas *you* in (48a) is produced by Raising-to-Object, and this difference is reflected in the difference of the grammaticality of (47b) and the ungrammaticality of (48b). Ross's analysis works, but not intuitively appealing in terms of practical usage.

A serious question is whether the full form and the deleted form have the same meaning/use. Since contraction is a type of deletion (i.e. partial deletion), the same question also applies to the contracted form. The matter of meaning preserving vs. changing between the full form and the deleted/contracted form will be dealt with in Unit 31.

Exercises and problems

1. Describe marking convention in detail.
2. Why is it that only unmarked objects can be deleted?
3. Why is it that the object case *that* in relative clauses are freely deleted, whereas *that* which is between the head noun and the content clause is not freely deleted?
4. Why is it that the sentential complementizer *that* can be deleted, if the main verb is non-factive?
5. Certain verbs allow *to-be* to be deleted. Do the verbs make a natural class?
6. Under what condition(s) can the sentential complementizer *that* be deleted in cleft sentences?

7. Fill in the blanks with the most appropriate expressions:

a. He tried (   ) a new book.

b. He tried (   ) the chocolate.

c. He tried (   ) the door.

d. She tried (   ) the pink dress

Unit 30

Contraction

Contraction may take place both at the lexical level and at the structural level.

Lexical Contraction

Lexical contraction has three types: acronyming, clipping, and blending. Acronyming means contraction where a letter represents a word or a morpheme. A contracted form (= an acronym) stands for the full form:

(1) a. IAEA = International Atomic Energy Agency
    b. msg = monosodium glutamine
    c. DNA = deoxyribonucleic acid
    d. UFO = unidentified flying object
    e. Y2K = year 2 kilo = year 2000

(2) a. BM = bowel movement
    b. Now, Cindy, dear. Grandma would like you to speak a bit more like a lady: Phydeaux didn't "shit the rug", he defecated on the carpet.
    c. . . . : Phydeaux didn't "shit the rug", he had a BM on the carpet.
    (Acronyms are euphemistic, e.g. SOB.)

Clipping is to clip part of a word:

(3) a. logo = logogram/logograph
 b. typo = typographic error
 c. Big Ben = Big Benjamin
 d. rec center = recreation center

Blending is to blend parts of two or more words:

(4) a. cybernation = cybernetic automation
 b. RAND = research and development
 c. Camford, Oxbridge = Cambridge and Oxford,
 Oxford and Cambridge
 d. bestore = best store

(5) A: What do you want to be, if you're reborn?
 B: a. I want to be a "liger" (= lion + tiger).
 b. I want to be a "huger" (= human + tiger).
 c. I want to be a "hugle" (= human + eagle).

Structural Contraction

Copula *be* can be contracted and attached to the preceding word. This is called "*be*-contraction". As usual, the *be*-contraction is subject to some constraint:

(6) a. I don't know where Bill is.
 b. *I don't know where Bill's.

(7) a. I wonder what time the concert is.
 b. *I wonder what time the concert's.

(8) a. I'm ready to help you.
b. Ready I am to help you.
c. *Ready I'm to help you.

(9) a. John is taller than Bill is.
b. *John's taller than Bill's.

(10) a. Tell Harry that the concert's at two.
b. *Tell Harry where the concert's at two.

As shown in the starred sentences above, the *be*-contraction is subject to some constraint. How can we generalize the constraint? I will posit the following hypothesis:

(11) Hypothesis A for the *be*-contraction
a. Structural/Formal: The *be*-contraction is prohibited if a gap has taken place in the adjacent environment.
b. Functional: The *be*-contraction is prohibited if there is already some information gap.

The essence of hypothesis A is this: double gap (i.e. a full gap and a full gap, or a full gap and a partial gap) in the adjacent environment is not allowed. Hypothesis A can account for the data in (6–10).

Let us test whether hypothesis A can also account for the "conjunctor-*be*" contraction:

(12) a. John has a house in Paris, but is living in London.
b. *John has a house in Paris, but's living in London.

(13) a. John's robbery means: John has robbed, or is robbed.
b. *John's robbery means: John has robbed, or's robbed.

(14) a. John was married yesterday and is leaving on his honeymoon trip.

b. *John was married yesterday and's leaving on his honeymoon trip.

(15) a. More beer is manufactured than is consumed.
b. *More beer is manufactured than's consumed.

Here again hypothesis A can account for data (12–15).

Next, let us test whether hypothesis A can also account for the *want-to* contraction: *want-to* may become [wəna]:

(16) Bill is the man I want to succeed. (ambiguous)
a. I want the man to succeed.
b. I want to succeed the man.

Sentence (16) is ambiguous between (a) and (b). Whether the sequence of *want to* can be contracted to [wəna] or not depends on the meaning. It can be contracted only for the meaning of (16b) because there is no gap in the adjacent environment. It cannot be contracted for the meaning of (16a), because there is a gap in the adjacent environment. Thus, hypothesis A can also account for the *want-to* contraction, which is also exemplified in the following:

(17) a. Which wine do you want to drink?
b. Who do you want to drink the wine?

(18) You can adopt a child if you want to.

In (17a), *want-to* can be contracted because there is no gap in the adjacent environment. In (17b), in contrast, *want-to* cannot be contracted, because there is a gap. In (18), *want-to* cannot be contracted, because there is a gap caused by VP Deletion.

Next let us test whether hypothesis A can account for the *have-to* contraction: *have-to* may become [hæfta]:

(19) What does John have to eat? (ambiguous)

a. John has bananas to eat.

b. John has to eat bananas.

Sentence (19) is ambiguous between (a) and (b). The sequence of *have-to* can be contracted to [hæfta] for the sense of (19b), because there is no gap . It cannot be contracted for the sense of (19a), because there is a gap. Hypothesis A can also account for the *have* contraction and the *supposed-to* contraction, which I will not illustrate here.

As raised in Unit 29, a serious question is whether the full form and the contracted form have the same meaning/use. The matter of meaning preserving vs. changing will be dealt with in Unit 31.

Exercises an problems

1. Specify each type of lexical contraction.
2. Describe the difference of deletion and contraction.
3. What type of lexical contraction is involved in *1st* and *2nd*?
4. *1999* can be clipped to *'99*. What about *2000*?
5. *That is* and *it is* can be contracted to *that's* and *it's*, respectively. How about *this is*?
6. *You would* can be contracted to *you'd*. And *you'd have* can be further contracted to *you'd've*. Is this against hypothesis A? If not, why not?
7. Why is it that *are* should be stressed in the following sentence? Generalize this phenomenon.

He's taller than you are.

8. Like *want-to* → [wəna] and twenty → [tweni], *can't* may become *can*. Why is it?
9. Is (c) acceptable? If not, why not?
   a. You may have this car if you want to have it.
   b. You may have this car if you want to.
   c. You may have this car if you wəna.

Unit 31

Meaning Preserving vs. Changing

If a rule optionally applies to a source sentence/form, two alternative sentences/forms are available: the source sentence/form and the derived sentence/form. In connection with this process, a serious problem arises: whether the two related sentences/forms have the same meaning or not. If they have the same meaning, the rule is meaning preserving. Otherwise, the rule is meaning changing. If the two sentences/forms have totally different meanings, they cannot be linked by transformational rules. They have their own sources. On the other hand, if two sentences/forms have totally or partially the same meaning, one sentence/form is the source sentence/form, and the other is derived from the source by a transformational rule.

Here, the important notion is synonymy. It is divided into (i) full synonymy, (ii) cognitive synonymy, and (iii) partial synonymy. Full synonymy is rarely available. Hence, any rule is meaning changing in terms of full synonymy. Rules are meaning preserving in terms of cognitive synonymy, which means that if one sentence is true, the other related sentence is also true, and conversely. For instance, an active sentence and its passive sentence have only cognitive synonymy, but not full synonymy. That is, two related sentences linked by a grammatical rule are cognitively synonymous. Thus, alternative expressibility is realized by knowing grammatical rules, which relate source sentences/forms to their derived sentences/forms, keeping cognitive synonymy. Foreign/second language learners are required to know rules, which produce alternative sentences.

If foreign/second language learners are satisfied with cognitive synonymy, they remain foreigners. On the other hand, if they want to become near-native speakers of the target language, they are required to know even partial synonymy. That is, they must know difference as well as similarity of the related sentences/forms. Partial synonymy, which means that two formally related or unrelated sentences/forms have subtle difference in meaning/use, occurs in two different contexts: (i) transformationally unrelated (t-unrelated, for short) sentences/forms, and (ii) transformationally related (t-related, for short) sentences/forms. For example:

(1) a. Smoking is illegal.
    b. Smoking is unlawful.

(2) a. He is polite to me.
    b. He is civil to me.

(3) a. Stop it!
    b. Don't do it!

(4) A: May I speak to Mrs. Smith?
    B: a. She is out.
       b. She is away.

In these examples, the (a) sentences and the (b) sentences have partial synonymy, which is very important for English learners to know. They are, however, t-unrelated. Hence, partial synonymy which occurs in t-unrelated sentences/forms is not the subject of this book. That requires another book, *English Semantics*, which must be designed for foreign/second language learners.

There are numberless pairs of sentences, which have subtlely different meanings although they look semantically same. For example,

(5) a. He forgot to take his medicine.
b. He forgot taking his medicine.

The formal difference is: (5a) has an infinitival complement object, and (5b) has a gerundival complement object. To foreigners, they look the same semantically. However, they have different meanings. In (5a), he didn't take his medicine, indicating its non-factual status (i.e. He forgot that he should take it), whereas in (5b), he did take his medicine, indicating its past "actually happened" status (i.e. He forgot that he had taken his medicine.) (cf. Yule 1998:216).

The similar difference can be seen in the following from Dixon (1991:170):

(6) a. John tried to eat the cake.
b. John tried eating the cake.

(7) a. John tried to travel by train.
b. John tried traveling by train.

The (a) sentences indicate that John wanted to engage in the activity, but may well not have been able to. In contrast, the (b) sentences indicate that John did engage in it for a sample period of time.

Meaning differences such as those of (5–7) are very important for foreign/second language learners of English to master it. This unit, however, does not deal with such pairs, simply because they are t-unrelated.

Since this book deals with grammatical rules which preserve cognitive synonymy, but may trigger partial synonymy, this unit deals with partial synonymy which occurs in t-related sentences/forms.

Now concrete illustrations are in order. In any preposing rule, the preposed element is emphasized. Hence, the source sentence and its derived (i.e. preposed) sentence have partial synonymy. That is, the two t-related sentences have the same meaning, except for emphasis. I do not illustrate them here.

Consider the following:

(8) a. The pencil pierced through the cushion.
    b. The pencil pierced the cushion through. (by Particle Movement)

(9) a. I taught my students humor.
    b. I taught humor to my students. (by Dative Shift)

(10) a. John sold Tom his Caxton Bible
     b. John sold his Caxton Bible to Tom. (by Dative Shift)
     (Dixon 1991:113-114)

(8a) connotes mere activity, while (8b) connotes achievement. (9a) connotes achievement, while (9b) does not. In the case of Dative Shift, Green (1974) emphasizes the semantic difference between the two versions. Dixon (1991:113–114) accords with Green's claim. According to Dixon, (10a) is appropriate in the context: Tom begs to be allowed to purchase the Bible; John doesn't need to sell it but he likes Tom and is prepared to oblige him. (10b) is appropriate in the context: John wants to sell his Bible to raise money. This is a very interesting contrast, which might not be recognized by ordinary speakers of English.

Raising-to-Object may also change meaning:

(11) a. I expect that John will help elderlies.
     b. I expect John to help elderlies. (by Raising-to-Object)
     (Dixon 19991:128)

(12) a. I heard that John had cursed.
 b. I heard John curse. (by Raising-to-Object)
 c. I heard John's cursing.

In (11), the possibility for John to help elderlies is higher in (11b) than in (11a). In (12a), I heard the information indirectly, and in (12b), I heard the information directly. (12c) is the same as (12b).

Deletion may also change meaning:

(13) a. John helped Mary to eat the pudding.
 b. John helped Mary eat the pudding.
 (Dixon 1991:199)

(14) a. John helped Sue to get into the car.
 b. John helped Sue get into the car.
 c. John helped Sue into the car.

According to Dixon (1991:199), in (13a), the helper made things easy for the helpee so that the helpee could do what needed to be done, whereas in (13b), the helper did part of the activity. In (14), the helper's effort is least in (a), maximal in (c), and in-between in (b).

The data in (13) and (14) can be generalized. Traditionally known causative verbs such as *let*, *make*, *have*, and *help* (excluding *cause* itself) have bare infinitives for their infinitive object complements. This is not accidental, because the causer's effort is maximal, while the causee's effort is minimal, in such causative sentences. In fact, the verb *help* is a causative or a non-causative because the relative efforts of the helper (= causer) and the helpee (= causee) are varied, including (14). Hence, the presence or absence of the infinitival complementizer *to* is not accidental: *help* in (14a) is a non-causative verb, and *help* in (14b) is a causative verb (cf. Yang 1999e).

We see the similar difference in the following data:

(15) a. John pushed Susan to get into the car.
b. John pushed Susan get into the car.
c. John pushed Susan into the car.

The causer's (= *John*) function is relatively maximal in (15c), relatively minimal in (15a), and in-between in (15b).

Possessive Deletion may also change meaning:

(16) a. *I appreciate you.
b. I appreciate your appreciation.
c. I appreciate your helping elderlies.
d. I appreciate you helping elderlies.

The contrast of (16a) and (16b) shows that the verb *appreciate* does not select human NPs for its object; it selects some activity for its object. Nonetheless, sentence (16d) is grammatical. This is not accidental. Sentence (16d) is derived from sentence (16c), where the object is an activity, by Possessive Deletion (which deletes the possessive of the gerund object NP). (16c) and (16d) have partial synonymy, but not full synonymy. In (16c), my appreciation is focused on one's activity, namely, your helping elderlies. In (16d), in contrast, my appreciation is focused on the person, namely, you. This contrast generally holds, which is also exemplified in the following:

(17) a. I am angry at the boy student's harassing the girl student.
b. I am angry at the boy student harassing the girl student.

In (17a), my anger is focused on the boy student's activity (i.e. harassing).

In (17b), in contrast, my anger is focused on the boy student.

Contraction may also change meaning:

(18) a. Let us go.
　　b. Let's go.

Concerning the persons involved in *let us* and *let's*, it is known that *let us* is ambiguous: (i) you and me, (ii) a third person(s) and me. In contrast, *let's* is not ambiguous: you and me. Pragmatically, however, *let's* is three ways ambiguous: (i) you and me, (ii) you alone, and (iii) me alone. The last two readings are illustrated in the following:

(19) a. (mommy to kid): Johnnie, let's wash hands.
　　b. (daddy to kids): Everyone, be quiet.
　　　Let's hear the phone message.

In (19a), the mother and her child both are involved, if she somehow helps him/her to wash hands. On the other hand, if the mother is just suggesting her child to wash hands, only the child is involved, which is based on Grice's (1975) cooperative principle. In the context of (19b), only the father is involved, which is based on Grice's cooperative principle.

Those simple examples show that even pragmatics, if necessary, must be invoked in understanding/analysing syntactic or semantic phenomena. The following examples dramatically demonstrate the need of pragmatics for the understanding/analysis of the negative imperatives of a special type:

(20) a. No spitting!
　　b. No smoking!
　　c. ?No farting!
　　d. ??No coughing!

e. * No sneezing!
f. ** No snoring!

The difference of acceptability of these negative imperative sentences is the very reflection of the difference of pragmatic controllability (cf. Yang 1998:33–34). We can control spitting or smoking, but even a superman cannot control snoring. One cannot make grammatical judgements on those sentences without knowing pragmatic information. For example, we can judge that sentence (20f) is worse than sentence (20e) because we know that snoring is much harder to control than sneezing, through our experiences.

Consider the following greetings:

(21) a. How are you doing?
b. How do you do?
c. How are you?
d. Howdy! (contracted form from (b))
e. Hi!

All of these sentences can be used for the same purpose, namely, greetings. All of them are cognitively synonymous. But they are partially synonymous since they have different degrees of formality/politeness. An interesting universal principle is: "the longer, the more formal, the more polite".

It should be noted that the principle indicated above does not necessarily imply that the longer forms are always recommended for politeness. It is questionable whether longer forms are necessarily more polite in the following examples from Bolinger (1977:5–6):

(22) Q: Who might have cut my hair better than John might have cut it?
A: a. Joe might have cut it better than John might have cut it.

b. Joe might have cut it better than John might have.
c. Joe might have cut it better than John might.
d. Joe might have cut it better than John.
e. Joe might have cut it better.
f. Joe might have.
g. Joe might.
h. Joe.

It seems that the principle may work among the (22e–h) versions. But it is questionable whether the principle works among the (22a–d) versions.

Thus far, I have shown that t-related sentences/forms usually have partial synonymy as well as cognitive synonymy. Such examples are numberless; the examples shown above are just samples. If foreign/second language learners of English want to become near-native speakers, they are required to master partial synonymy of all kinds: partial synonymy which occurs between t-unrelated as well as t-related sentences/forms. For this purpose, Bolinger's work, Dixon's work and Fillmore's work, among others, are good guidelines. If this goal is too tough to achieve, then foreign/second language learners of English must be satisfied with mastering cognitive synonymy, which occurs between source sentences and their derived sentences. This book is designed to satisfy the English learners of the second category. (This paragraph may be regarded as the conclusion of this book.)

Exercises and problems

1. Define "cognitive" synonymy and "partial" synonymy.
2. In meaning, is (c) closer to (a) or (b)?

a. John helped Mary to finish her thesis.

b. John helped Mary finish her thesis.

c. Mary was helped (by John) to finish her thesis.

Discuss whether *help* in (a) a causative verb or a non-causative verb.

3. The verb *push* may be used in a physical sense or in a mental sense. Under what condition can *push* be used in a mental sense?
4. Under what condition can the verb *appreciate* take human objects?
5. Specify Grice's "cooperative principle". How does it affect syntactic phenomena?

REFERENCES

Abbott, Barbara. 1976. Right Node Raising as a Test for Constituenthood. *Linguistic Inquiry* 7.4: 639–642.

Akmajian, Adrian and Frank Heny. 1975. *An Introduction to the Principles of Transformational Syntax*. MIT Press.

Bach, Emmon. 1974. *Syntactic Theory*. New York: HRW.

Baker, Carl L. 1978. *Introduction to Generative-Transformational Syntax*. Englewood Cliffs: Prentice-Hall.

Bolinger, Dwight. 1971. *The Phrasal Verb in English*. Harvard University Press.

_____________. 1977. *Meaning and Form*. London: Longman.

Borkin, Ann. 1984. *Problems in Form and Function*. Norwood, New Jersey: Ablex.

Brame, Michael K. 1979. *Essays Toward Realistic Syntax*. Seattle: Noit Amrofer.

_______________. 1980. Hope. *Linguistic Analysis* 6.3: 247–259.

Bresnan, Joan W. 1974. The Position of Certain Clause-particles in Phrase Structure. *Linguistic Inquiry* 5.4: 614–619.

Cattell, Ray. 1973. Negative Transportation and Tag Questions. *Language* 49.3: 612–639.

Channon, Robert. 1975. Acceptable Ambiguity. *BLS* 1: 37–46.

Chomsky, Noam. 1965. *Aspects of the Theory of Syntax*. MIT Press.

Clark, Eve V. and Herbert H. Clark. 1979. When Nouns Surface as Verbs. *Language* 55.4: 767–811.

Collins, Peter. 1991. *Cleft and Pseudo-Cleft Constructions in English*. London: Routledge.

Culicover, Peter. 1982. *Though*-Attraction. IULC.

Davison, Alice. 1980. Peculiar Passives. *Language* 56.1: 42–66.

Dixon, Robert M.W. 1991. *A New Approach to English Grammar on Semantic Principles*. Oxford: Clarendon Press.

Ducrot, Oswald. 1972. *Dire et Ne Pas Dire.* Paris: Hermann.

Emonds, Joseph E. 1972. A Reformulation of Certain Syntactic Transformations. In Peters (1972).

______________. 1976. *A Transformational Approach to English Syntax.* New York: Academic Press.

Engdahl, Elisabet. 1983. Parasitic Gaps. *Linguistics and Philosophy* 6.1: 5–34.

Fagan, Sarah M. B. 1988. The English Middle. *Linguistic Inquiry* 19.2: 181–204.

Fillmore, Charles J. 1986. Pragmatically Controlled Zero Anaphora. *BLS* 12: 95–107.

Fillmore, Charles J., Paul Kay, and Mary Catherine O'Conner. 1988. Regularity and Idiomaticity in Grammatical Constructions. *Language* 64.3: 501–538.

Fillmore, Charles J. and Paul Kay. 1993. *Construction Grammar.* University of California, Berkeley. Ms.

Fraser, Bruce. 1974. *The Verb-Particle Combination in English.* Tokyo: Taishukan Publishing Co.

Goldberg, Adele E. 1992. The Inherent Semantics of Argument Structure: The Case of the English Ditransitive Construction. *Cognitive Linguistics* 3.1: 37–74.

______________. 1995. *Constructions: A Construction Grammar Approach to Argument Structure.* University of Chicago Press.

Goldsmith, John. 1985. A Principled Exception to the Coordinate Structure Constraint. *CLS* 21: 133–143.

Green, Georgia M. 1974. *Semantics and Syntactic Regularity.* Indiana University Press.

______________. 1980. Some Wherefores of English Inversions. *Language* 56.3: 582–601.

Grice, H. Paul. 1975. Logic and Conversation. In *Speech Acts: Syntax and Semantics* 3, ed. by Peter Cole and Jerry L. Morgan, 41–58. New York: Academic Press.

Grimshaw, Jane. 1979. Complement Selection and the Lexicon. *Linguistic Inquiry* 10.2: 279–326.

Grosu, Alexander. 1972. The Strategic Nature of Island Constraints. *Ohio State University Working Papers in Linguistics* 13: 1–25.

Gundel, Jeanette K. 1977. Where Do Cleft Sentences Come From? *Language* 53.3: 543–559.

Haiman, John. 1985. *Natural Syntax*. Cambridge University Press.

Hankamer, Jorge. 1971. *Constraints on Deletion in Syntax*. Doctoral Dissertation, Yale University.

______________. 1973. Unacceptable Ambiguity. *Linguistic Inquiry* 4.1: 17–68.

Hooper, Joan B. 1975. On Assertive Predicates. *Syntax and Semantics*, vol. 4. New York: Academic Press.

Horn, Laurence R. 1985. Metalinguistic Negation and Pragmatic Ambiguity. *Language* 61.1: 121–174.

Huck, Geoffrey J. and Younghee Na. 1990. Extraposition and Focus. *Language* 66.1: 51–77.

Jackendoff, Ray S. 1977. *X-bar Syntax*. MIT Press.

________________. and Peter Culicover. 1971. A Reconsideration of Dative Movements. *Founda- tions of Language* 7.3: 397–412.

Jacobs, Roderick A. 1975. Promotion and Thematization Process in English. *CLS Functionalism.*

Jacobson, Paulin. 1990. Raising as Function Composition. *Linguistics and Philosophy* 13.4: 423–475.

Jake, Janice. 1977. Gapping, Pragmatics, and Factivity. *CLS* 13.

Jespersen, Otto. 1927. *A Modern English Grammar on Historical Principles*, vol. 3. London: George Allen and Unwin.

Keyser, Samuel J. and Thomas Roeper. 1984. On the Middle and Ergative Constructions. *Linguistic Inquiry* 15.3: 381–416.

Kim, Young-Wha, Kim Il-Kon, and Park Jeong-Woon (eds.). 1999. *Linguistic Investigations in Honor of Professor In-Seok Yang*. Seoul: hankook Publishing Co.

Kiparsky, Paul and Carol Kiparsky. 1970. Fact. In *Progress in Linguistics*, ed. by Manfred Bierwisch and Karl E. Heidolph. The Hague: Mouton.

Kuno, Susumu. 1975. Conditions for VP Deletion. *Foundations of Language* 13.2: 161–175.

___________. 1976. Gapping: A Functional Analysis. *Linguistic Inquiry* 7.2: 300–318.

Lakoff, George. 1970. Pronominalization, Negation, and the Analysis of Adverbs. In *Readings of English Transformational Grammar*, ed. by Roderick Jacobs and Peter Rosenbaum. Waltham, Massachusetts: Ginn and Co.

___________. 1973. Some Thoughts on Transderivational Constraints. In *Issues in Linguistics*, ed by Braj B Kachru *et al.* University of Illinois Press.

___________. 1986. *Women, Fire, and Dangerous Things*. University of Chicago Press.

___________ and John Ross. 1976. Why You Can't *Do So* into the Sink. *Syntax and Semantics*, vol. 7, 101-111. New York: Academic Press.

Lakoff, Robin. 1969. A Syntactic Argument for Negative Transportation. *CLS* 5: 140–147.

Larson, Richard K. 1988. On the Double Object Construction. *Linguistic Inquiry* 19.3: 335–391.

Lasnik, Howard and Robert Fiengo. 1974. Complement Object Deletion. *Linguistic Inquiry* 5.4: 535–571.

Leech, Geoffrey. 1983. Principles of Pragmatics. London: Longman.

Lees, Robert B. 1960. *The Grammar of English Nominalizations*. The Hague: Mouton.

Li, Charles N. (ed.). 1976. *Subject and Topic*. New York: Academic Press.

McCawley, James D. 1988. *The Syntactic Phenomena of English*, vols. 1 and 2. University of Chicago Press.

Maling, Joan M. 1976. Notes on Quantifier-Postposing. *Linguistic Inquiry* 7.4: 708–718.

Michaelis, Laura A. and Knud Lambrecht. 1996. Toward a Construction-based Theory of Language Function: The Case of Nominal Extraposition. *Language* 72.2: 215–247.

Mittwoch, Anita. 1982. On the Difference between *Eating* and *Eating Something*: Activities vs. Accomplishments. *Linguistic Inquiry* 13.1: 113–122.

Nanni, Debora L. 1980. On the Surface Syntax of Constructions with *Easy*-type

Adjectives. *Language* 56.3: 568–581.

Peters, Stanley (ed.). *Goals of Linguistic Theory.* Englewood Cliffs, New Jersey: Prentice-Hall.

Pope, Emily N. 1975. *Questions and Answers in English.* IULC.

Postal, Paul M. 1971. *Cross-over Phenomena.* New York: HRW.

____________. 1974. *On Raising.* MIT Press.

____________. 1994. Parasitic and Pseudo-parasitic Gaps. *Linguistic Inquiry* 25.1: 63–117.

Prince, Ellen F. 1981. Topicalization, Focus-Movement, and Yiddish-Movement. *BLS* 7: 249–264.

Quirk, Randolph, Sidney Greenbaum, Geoffrey Leech, and Jan Svartvik. 1985. *A Comprehensive Grammar of the English Language.* London: Longman.

Reinhart, Tanya. 1982. Pragmatics and Linguistics: An Analysis of Sentence Topics. IULC

Rosenbaum, Peter S. 1967. *The Grammar of English Predicate Complement Constructions.* MIT Press.

Ross, John Robert. 1969. Guess Who? *CLS* 5: 252–286.

_______________. 1973a. Nouniness. In *Three Dimensions of Linguistic Theory,* ed by Osamu Fujimura, 139-257. Tokyo: TEC.

_______________. 1973b. Slifting. In *The Formal Analysis of Natural Languages,* ed by Maurice Gross, Morris Halle, and Marcel-Paul Schuetzenberg. The Hague: Mouton.

_______________. 1986. *Infinite Syntax.* Norwood, New Jersey: Ablex.

Sadler, Louisa and Douglas J. Arnold 1994. Prenominal Adjectives and the Phrasal/ Lexical Distinction. *Journal of Linguistics* 30: 187–226.

Sag, Ivan A. 1978. Floating Quantifiers, Adverbs, and Extraction Sites. *Linguistic Inquiry* 9.1: 146–150.

___________. 1983. On Parasitic Gaps. *Linguistics and Philosophy* 6.1: 35–45.

Sells, Peter. 1984. *Syntax and Semantics of Resumptive Pronouns.* Doctoral Dissertation, University of Massachusetts.

___________. 1985. *Lectures on Contemporary Syntactic Theories.* Stanford: CSLI.

Siegel, Dorothy. 1973. Nonsources of *Un*-passives. *Syntax and Semantics*, vol 2: 301–317.

Swan, Michael. 1995. *Practical English Usage*. Oxford University Press.

Sweetser, Eve. 1990. *From Etymology to Pragmatics.* Cambridge University Press.

Thompson, Sandra A. 1971. The Deep Structure of Relative Clauses. In *Studies in Linguistic Semantics,* ed. by Charles J. Fillmore and D. Terence Langendoen. New York: HRW.

Thomson, A. J. and A. V. Martinet. 1980. *A Practical English Grammar*. Oxford University Press.

van Dongen Sr., W. A. 1919. He Puts on His Hat and He Puts His Hat on. *Neophilosogus* 4: 322–353.

van Oosten, Jeanne. 1977. Subjects and Agenthhod in English. *CLS* 13: 459–471.

Vendler, Zeno. 1967. *Linguistics in Philosophy*. Cornell University Press.

Visser, F. Th. 1973. *A Historial Syntax of the English Language*, vol. III.2. Leiden: E. J. Brill.

Ward, Gregory L. 1990. The Discourse Function of VP Preposing. *Language* 66.4: 742–763.

Wierzbicka, Anna. 1982. Why Can You *Have a Drink* When You Can't **Have an Eat*? *Language* 58.4: 753–799.

Wood, Frederick T. 1955. Verb-adverb Combinations: The Position of Adverbs. *English Language Teaching* 10: 18–27.

Yang, In-Seok. 1972. *Korean Syntax*. Seoul: Paehapsa.

____________. 1993. *Linguistic Explorations: Syntax, Semantics and Pragmatics.* Seoul: Hanshin Publishing Co.

____________. 1993a. Remarks on English VP Preposing. In Yang (1993).

____________. 1993b. Subject-Verb Inversions in English. In Yang (1993).

____________. 1993c. Scale-point Negation. In Yang (1993).

____________. 1993d. More on Content Clauses. In Yang (1993).

____________. 1993e. *Like* or *Unlike*? The Y-Ambiguity in English. In Yang (1993).

____________. 1993f. The Semantics and Pragmatics of Antonymy: Neutralizability and Implication. In Yang (1993).

__________. 1993g. Condition and Concession. In Yang (1993).

__________. 1995. On the Surface Verb *Remain* and *Un*-passives. *Korean Journal of Linguistics* 20.4: 143–158.

__________. 1998. *Welcome Aboard the Humor Pleasure Boat*. Seoul: hankook Publishing Co.

__________. 1999a. Special Passives and Affection. Ms.

__________. 1999b. Beneficiary Datives and Lexical Decomposition. Ms.

__________. 1999c. Korean Denominal Verbs. *Korean Journal of Linguistics* 24/2: 291-310.

__________. 1999d. Why Rre **Why to* and **Whyever* Impossible? Ms.

__________. 1999e. Causative Verbs in English. Ms.

Yule, George. 1998. *Explaining English Grammar*. Oxford University Press.

INDEX

Q

R

S